THE LORD OF THE RINGS

Comprehension Guide
by Alyameldir,
son of Meldarion
—a Bustard

www.VeritasPress.com
(800) 922-5082

This guide is dedicated to my dear friend
Stephen R. Smith in thanks for introducing me to the realm
of Arda and for his good fellowship over the years.

First Edition 2007

Veritas Press

Copyright ©2007 Veritas Press
www.VeritasPress.com
(800) 922-5082
ISBN 978-1-932168-71-6

All rights reserved. Permission is granted to make unlimited photocopies of this entire manual for the school or homeschool that purchased this manual. Otherwise, no part of this book may be reproduced without permission from Veritas Press, except by a reviewer who may quote brief passages in a review; nor may any part of this book be reproduced, stored in a retrieval system or transmitted in any form by any means, electronic, mechanical, photocopying, recording or otherwise, without prior permission from Veritas Press.
Printed in the United States of America.

THE LORD OF THE RINGS
How to use this Guide

This guide is intended to help you study, understand, and enjoy *The Lord of the Rings*. You might ask if a guide is really necessary to read a book. Is the student not just working to improve reading skills while being taught to enjoy reading a book? Certainly, it is the case that the more a child reads, the more he should improve his skills, but quantity is not the only issue. Once a child has received adequate phonetic training he should learn how to read a book. Most educators using this guide will be teaching children in the grammar stage, generally understood to be during the elementary years in a classical education. (For a thorough understanding of classical Christian education we recommend reading *Recovering the Lost Tools of Learning* or *The Case for Classical Christian Education*, both by Douglas Wilson.) The basic goals of reading in the grammar stage are as follows:

The student should be able to:
1. Fluently read a given selection orally.
2. Show an increased desire for reading.
3. Show comprehension on a literal and inferential level.
4. Demonstrate an increased vocabulary.
5. Identify basic Biblical values in the literature being read.
6. Identify various styles (myths, poems, fantasy, fiction, nonfiction, etc.)

Answers to the questions are found in the back of the guide. The students' answers should be in complete sentences, and they should restate the question in their answer.

Example:

Question: Whose birthdays are on September 22nd?

Answer: September 22nd is the birthday of Bilbo Baggins and his nephew Frodo Baggins.

Such writing practice trains the student to answer thoroughly, completely, and with proper grammar. Another reason is to encourage integration. We want students to understand that how they write something is as important as what they write. After the grammar stage, students enter the dialectic stage, where they develop an interest in logic, analysis and critical thinking. *The Lord of the Rings* is a good work to start transitioning students into this stage.

You may wonder how to grade the student's work in this guide. Keep it simple. Unless otherwise indicated you should assume that each question is worth five points.

Note: At the time of printing there is a blog (http://tolkiengeek.blogspot.com) which may serve teachers well as it provides overviews for each chapter.

ALL, ONE RING TO FIND THEM, ONE RING TO RULE THEM
TO BRING THEM ALL AND IN THE DARKNESS

THREE RINGS
FOR THE ELVEN
KINGS UNDER THE
SKY, SEVEN FOR THE
DWARF LORDS IN
THEIR HALLS OF STONE, NINE
FOR MORTAL MEN DOOMED
TO DIE, ONE FOR THE
DARK LORD ON HIS DARK
THRONE IN THE LAND OF
MORDOR WHERE THE
SHADOWS LIE.   ONE RING TO RULE THEM
AND IN THE DARKNESS
BIND THEM.

IN THE LAND OF MORDOR
WHERE THE SHADOWS LIE.
            —J.R.R. TOLKIEN

THE LORD OF THE RINGS: BOOK ONE
A Long Expected Party

1. Whose birthdays are on September 22nd?

   _____

   _____

2. What was the fate of Drogo Baggins?

   _____

   _____

3. Along with stories of elves and dragons, what did Sam Gamgee learn from the owner of Bag End?

   _____

   _____

   _____

4. To what was the fame of Gandalf in the Shire due?

   _____

   _____

5. Why did everyone who came to the party receive a present?

   _____

   _____

   _____

6. How many hobbits were invited to the special meal under the pavillion?

   _____

   _____

   _____

7. After the feast what three purposes were given as the reason for the assembly?

_____

_____

_____

8. Often described as "well-preserved," how did Bilbo describe the way he felt to Gandalf?

_____

_____

_____

9. What did Gandalf especially want to make sure was left behind for Frodo?

_____

_____

_____

10. What did Bilbo call the object—which once was kept by Gollum—that startled and alarmed Gandalf?

_____

_____

_____

11. Though most things that were marked to be given away the following day went where they were most wanted and welcome, what were given to the following hobbits, and what was Biblo saying in a humourous or pointed way with each present?

    Adelard Took's gift: _____

       The meaning of Adelard's gift: _____

    Dora Baggins's gift: _____

       The meaning of Dora's gift: _____

    Milo Burrows's gift: _____

       The meaning of Milo's gift: _____

    Angelica Baggins's gift: _____

       The meaning of Angelica's gift: _____

    Hugo Bracegirdle's gift: _____

       The meaning of the gift: _____

    Lobelia Sackville-Baggins's gift: _____

       The meaning of the gift: _____

12. Before taking his leave and saying, "Look out for me, especially at unlikely times!" what last words of warning did Gandalf give to Frodo about Gollum's old "present?"

    _____

    _____

    _____

THE LORD OF THE RINGS: BOOK ONE
Project—Party Invitations

Write an invitation to Bilbo's party in calligraphy to look like the hobbit's own handwriting. If you have experience in calligraphy, you will notice it is very similar to the majuscule script Uncial. Following is an example of what you might write. Remember to include the location and any other details you can glean from the chapter. The lines on the next page are for you to use to practice, before writing on a nice sheet of paper. Draw lines faintly in pencil as guides, then erase them when your invitation is complete.

you are cordially invited
on the twenty-second of september,
to the eleventy-first birthday
of bilbo, son of bungo baggins
and belladonna took.
fireworks will be provided
by gandalf the grey.
the party will be held under ...

THE LORD OF THE RINGS: BOOK ONE
Project—Party Invitations

a b c d e f g h i j k l m n o p q r s t u v w x y z

THE LORD OF THE RINGS: BOOK ONE
The Shadow of the Past

1. What odd and unusual custom did Frodo keep year after year?

   _____

   _____

2. What were the names of some of Frodo's friends?

   _____

   _____

3. What news was Frodo able to glean from Elves traveling west and Dwarves on their way to the Blue
   Mountains?

   _____

   _____

   _____

4. What did Sam report one evening at the Green Dragon,
   during the spring of Frodo's fiftieth year, that his cousin
   saw in the North Moors?

   _____

   _____

   _____

5. Who was Saruman?

   _____

   _____

   _____

6. After it was removed from the fire, what did Frodo see on the ring and what did Gandalf say it meant about the ring?

_____

_____

7. Why did Sauron the Great, the Dark Lord, want to recover Frodo's ring?

_____

_____

_____

_____

8. Who helped Gandalf track Gollum the whole length of Wilderland?

_____

_____

_____

9. Why did the ring cause Bilbo so little hurt from evil and make it possible to escape from owning it?

_____

_____

_____

10. What punishment did Gandalf inflict on Mr. Underhill's gardener for eavesdropping?

_____

_____

_____

THE LORD OF THE RINGS: BOOK ONE
Project 1–Paper Ring

Materials

scissors

glue stick

transparent tape

yellow marker

Directions

Choose which size ring you want and color it gold or yellow. Cut along the solid black line then fold on the dashed line (the top of the band is the inside of the ring). Use stick glue to seal the folded sides together then tape the ends together to complete the ring (you will probably need to trim off an end or two).

THE LORD OF THE RINGS: BOOK ONE
Project 2—History Writing

Rewrite in your own words how the Dark Lord first lost the One Ring and what happened to it afterwards.

_____

_____

_____

_____

_____

_____

_____

_____

_____

_____

_____

_____

_____

_____

_____

_____

_____

_____

_____

_____

_____

_____

THE LORD OF THE RINGS: BOOK ONE
Three is Company

1. To whom did Frodo sell Bag End?

   _____

   _____

2. What expected guest was missing from the Birthday Party at Bag End the year Frodo moved out?

   _____

   _____

   _____

3. What did Sam say a final farewell to at Bag End that had Frodo calling after him?

   _____

   _____

   _____

4. What came across Frodo, Sam and Pippin as they slept on their first night walking to Buckland that thought, "Hobbits! What next? I have heard of strange doings in this land, but I have seldom heard of a hobbit sleeping out of doors under a tree. Three of them!"

   _____

   _____

   _____

5. Bilbo used to tell his nephew, "It's a dangerous business, Frodo, going out of your door," and compared the Road to what?

   _____

   _____

   _____

THE LORD OF THE RINGS: BOOK ONE
Three is Company, Page 2

6. Describe the traveler that the hobbits hid from that Frodo described as "smelling" for him.

   _____

   _____

7. What is the name of the village near to which Gildor and his companions took the hobbits to spend the night?

   _____

8. What was the only information that Frodo was able to acquire from Gildor about Bilbo?

   _____

   _____

9. Why was it said: "Do not meddle in the affairs of Wizards . . ."?

   _____

   _____

10. Why was it said: "Go not to the Elves for counsel . . ."?

   _____

   _____

   _____

THE LORD OF THE RINGS: BOOK ONE
Project—Map

Photocopy this map at 120% on 11x17" paper and plot out the story while you read the Trilogy.

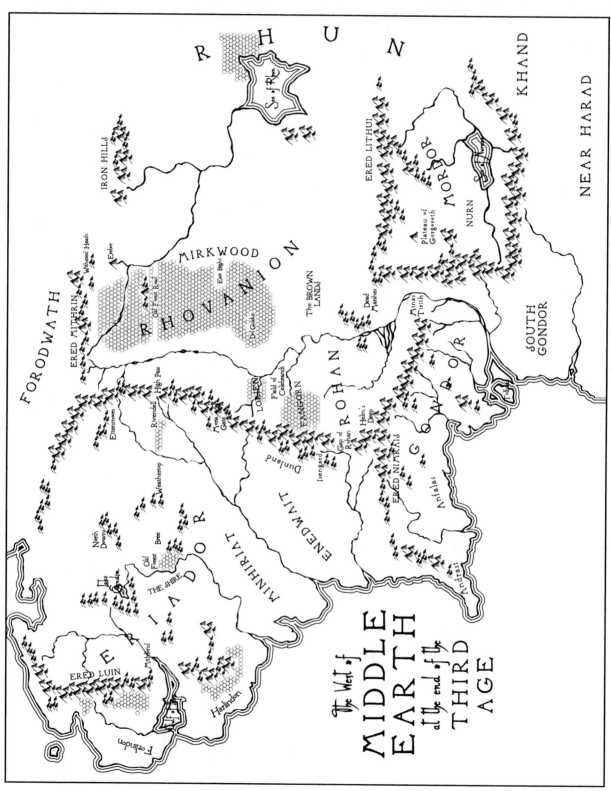

THE LORD OF THE RINGS: BOOK ONE
A Short Cut to Mushrooms and A Conspiracy Unmasked

1. Who surprised Frodo by describing the elves as, ". . . so old and young, and so gay and sad"?

_____

_____

_____

2. Pippin argued with Frodo that, "Short cuts make long delays." But what was the principle reason for him to object to Frodo's choice in course to reach Bucklebury Ferry?

_____

_____

_____

3. Why was Frodo terrified of Farmer Maggot?

_____

_____

_____

4. What news did the farmer give the three hobbits before asking them to stay for dinner?

_____

_____

_____

5. What parting gift did the farmer give to Frodo when they met up with Merry at the entrance to the Ferry lane?

_____

_____

_____

6. How were the Bucklanders different from other hobbits of the Shire?

_____

_____

7. What had "blessed Meriadoc" prepared for the travelers at Frodo's new house at Crickhollow?

_____

_____

_____

8. What, after a meal and an able serving of mushrooms, did Merry reveal to Frodo that left young Mr. Baggins speechless?

_____

_____

_____

9. Who was the Conspiracy's chief investigator and what advice from Gildor did he parrot back to Frodo which insured the addition of traveling companions on Frodo's journey?

_____

_____

_____

10. According to the original plans of the conspirators, what was Fatty Bolger's task?

THE LORD OF THE RINGS: BOOK ONE
Project 1—The Bath Song

Compose a new verse for Bilbo's favorite bathsong. Notice that the rhyming scheme is AABB and that each stanza ends with a comment about hot water.

> Sing hey! for the bath at close of day
> That washes the weary mud away!
> A loon is he that will not sing:
> O! Water Hot is a noble thing!
>
> O! Sweet is the sound of falling rain.
> and the brook that leaps from hill to plain;
> but better than rain or rippling streams
> is Water Hot that smokes and steams.
>
> O! Water cold we may pour at need
> down a thirsty throat and be glad indeed;
> but better is Beer, if drink we lack,
> and Water Hot poured down the back.
>
> O! Water is fair that leaps on high
> in a fountain white beneath the sky;
> but never did fountain sound so sweet
> as splashing Hot Water with my feet!

_____

_____

_____

_____

Hey, while you're at it, why not write another verse?

_____

_____

_____

_____

THE LORD OF THE RINGS: BOOK ONE
Project 2—Barley-Mushroom Soup

Ingredients

1 1/2 teaspoons olive oil

1 1/2 cups chopped onion

1 cup thinly sliced carrot

1 (8-ounce) package presliced mushrooms

1/2 cup uncooked pearl barley

4 3/4 cups rich turkey stock

1/3 cup finely chopped celery

1/2 teaspoon salt

1/2 teaspoon chopped fresh or 1/4 teaspoon dried thyme

Preparation

Heat the oil in a large saucepan over medium-high heat. Add onion, carrot, and mushrooms; sauté 7 minutes or until golden brown. Stir in barley, and sauté 2 minutes. Add stock, celery, and salt, and bring to a boil. Cover, reduce heat, and simmer 20 minutes. Add thyme and cook 5 minutes.

Yields 4 servings (serving size: 1 1/2 cups)

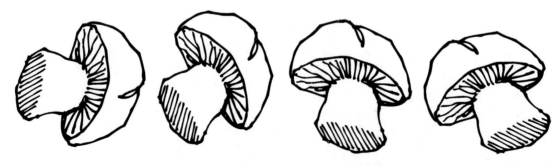

THE LORD OF THE RINGS: BOOK ONE
Project 3—Farfalle with Creamy Wild Mushroom Sauce

Ingredients

1 pound uncooked farfalle (bow tie pasta)

1 tablespoon butter

12 ounces presliced blend of shiitake, cremini, and oyster mushrooms

1/2 cup chopped onion

1/3 cup finely chopped shallots

1 tablespoon minced garlic

1 1/2 teaspoons salt, divided

1/4 teaspoon freshly ground black pepper

1/4 cup dry white wine

2/3 cup whipping cream

1/2 cup (2 ounces) grated fresh Parmigiano-Reggiano cheese

2 tablespoons chopped fresh parsley

Preparation

Cook pasta according to package directions, omitting salt and fat; drain. Melt the butter in a large nonstick skillet over medium-high heat. Add the mushrooms (you can use all cremini mushrooms if the others are not available), onion, shallots, garlic, 1 teaspoon salt, and pepper; cook 12 minutes or until liquid evaporates and mushrooms are tender, stirring occasionally. Add wine; cook 2 minutes or until liquid evaporates, stirring occasionally. Remove from heat. Add the cooked pasta, whipping cream, cheese, and 2 tablespoons parsley, tossing gently to coat. Stir in remaining 1/2 teaspoon salt. Serve immediately.

Yields 8 servings (serving size: 1 1/4 cups)

THE LORD OF THE RINGS: BOOK ONE
The Old Forest and In the House of Tom Bombadil

1. What did Merry say the Old Forest will do to wanderers during the day?

   _____

   _____

   _____

2. The Old Forest seemed to force them towards the Withywindle valley against the hobbits' wishes. What did the hobbits do to try to find refuge from the armies of flies and afternoon sun?

   _____

   _____

   _____

   _____

3. What did Old Man Willow try to do to Merry and Pippin?

   _____

   _____

4. Describe Tom Bombadil as he appeared to the hobbits on his way home from water-lily, green leaves and lily gathering.

   _____

   _____

   _____

5. Describe Goldberry as she first appeared to the hobbits.

   _____

   _____

   _____

THE LORD OF THE RINGS: BOOK ONE
The Old Forest and *In the House of Tom Bombadil, Page 2*

6. What was Goldberry doing while Tom told (and sang) lore of the Old Forest for the hobbits?

   _____

   _____

   _____

   _____

7. Besides telling them of bees and flowers, strange creatures of the Forest, and the ancient fathers of the trees, what did Tom tell them about which made the hobbits shudder?

   _____

   _____

   _____

   _____

8. What hobbit did Tom esteem and why?

_____

_____

_____

9. What happened to the Ring in Tom's hand? What effect did the Ring have on Tom when he put it on?

_____

_____

_____

_____

10. What warning did Tom repeatedly give the hobbits concerning their travels the following day?

_____

_____

_____

_____

THE LORD OF THE RINGS: BOOK ONE
Project—Why isn't Tom in the movie?

"And even in a mythical Age there must be some enigmas, as there always are. Tom Bombadil is one (intentionally)." —*The Letters of J. R. R. Tolkien*, No. 144.

Almost every part of Middle-earth Tolkien described in detail, but Tom Bombadil he left as a mystery. He is not a man or a hobbit, and although he loves song and is very wise, he is not elvish ("When the Elves passed westward, Tom was here already"). Some have proposed that Tom is of the Valar or the Maiar (beings discussed at length in *The Silmarillion*), and it has even been suggested that Tom—or Goldberry—are, in fact, the reader! Regardless of what he is, Tom is a beloved character by readers of *The Lord of the Rings*. In light of his broad appeal, it was a shock to many when Tom was *not* included in Peter Jackson's film trilogy (sorry for that spoiler!). *Write a short essay about why you think he had to be omitted. What is it about Tom that makes him hard to film and such an enigma?*

THE LORD OF THE RINGS: BOOK ONE
Fog on the Barrow-Downs

1. As the hobbits made their way towards the Brandywine River, what realization stopped Frodo in his tracks and distressed him so that he wanted to turn back?

   _____

   _____

   _____

2. What did the hobbits unintentionally do after lunch by the standing stone on the hilltop?

   _____

   _____

   _____

3. What happened to "the best hobbit in the Shire" when he was separated from the other hobbits?

   _____

   _____

   _____

4. What was laid across the necks of Merry, Pippin and Sam when Frodo found them?

   _____

   _____

5. After bravely hacking the crawling arm, what did Frodo do that saved the hobbits?

   _____

   _____

6. What was the effect of singing *"... Dark door is standing wide; dead hand is broken./Night under Night is flown, and the Gate is open!"*

_____

_____

_____

7. Who are Sharp-ears, Wise-nose, Swish-tail and Bumpkin?

_____

_____

8. How was the treasure from the mound divided?

_____

_____

_____

9. Where were the hobbits advised to stay, once they reached Bree?

_____

_____

10. What did Merry report concerning the type of people the hobbits would meet in Bree?

_____

_____

_____

THE LORD OF THE RINGS: BOOK ONE
Project—Barrow-Downs Word Search

Find the words listed at the bottom of the page in the word search below.

```
T  O  L  K  I  E  N  J  R  W  I  T  C  H  K
C  L  I  D  A  B  M  O  B  P  I  P  P  N  I
G  A  N  D  A  L  F  S  A  O  M  F  R  O  N
T  Y  R  N  G  O  R  T  H  A  D  M  E  R  G
E  G  O  N  D  O  R  E  L  F  U  O  X  W  L
Q  S  C  G  D  S  A  U  R  O  N  T  R  Y  I
R  M  S  X  D  U  N  E  D  A  I  N  D  F  C
T  I  E  E  D  M  D  D  D  D  D  D  D  D  A
W  O  N  R  N  A  L  O  D  R  A  C  D  D  I
I  N  O  G  Y  R  R  E  M  S  H  I  R  W  R
G  I  S  K  A  D  E  A  D  B  R  E  E  O  N
H  P  H  D  E  U  N  T  W  A  B  C  N  R  S
T  P  G  O  L  D  B  E  S  R  Y  R  F  R  E
Q  I  N  U  M  E  N  O  R  E  A  N  S  A  M
W  P  E  R  T  S  O  N  G  R  W  Y  K  B  J
```

MERRY	NÚMENÓREANS	WESTERNESSE
PIPPIN	ARNOR	CARN DUM
SAM	CARDOLAN	BOMBADIL
FRODO	DUNEDAIN	WIGHT
CAIRN	DEAD	SONG
BARROW	WITCH-KING	TYRN GORTHAD

THE LORD OF THE RINGS: BOOK ONE
At the Sign of the Prancing Pony and *Strider*

1. What did Bree-folk believe concerning the tall, dark wandering Rangers?

   _____

   _____

   _____

2. What relieved Sam's misgivings about staying at *The Prancing Pony?*

   _____

   _____

3. What did Frodo claim to be thinking of doing that got everyone talking to him?

   _____

   _____

4. Describe Strider's appearance.

   _____

   _____

   _____

   _____

5. What happened after the cow jumped over the moon?

   _____

   _____

   _____

6. What "reward" did Strider ask of Frodo in exchange for good advice?

_____

_____

_____

7. What did Butterbur deliver to a *perky chap with a bright eye* while the hobbits were debating the wisdom in giving Strider his "reward"?

_____

_____

_____

8. What was Strider's true name?

_____

9. What was unique about the weapon that Strider carries?

_____

_____

_____

10. What caused Merry to fall over and dream "an ugly dream"?

_____

_____

_____

THE LORD OF THE RINGS: BOOK ONE
A Knife in the Dark

1. Why was the Horn-call blown in Buckland?

   _____

   _____

   _____

2. Why were the hobbits able to have a good breakfast even though Strider had wanted to leave Bree early and quietly?

   _____

   _____

   _____

3. Mr. Butterbur bought a pony from Bill Ferny, paying three times more than the beast was worth. How did things come out right in the end for the innkeeper?

   _____

   _____

   _____

   _____

4. Sam declared that "Apples for walking, and a pipe for sitting." For what else did Sam find that apples were useful?

   _____

   _____

   _____

5. Where was it said that Elendil stood watching for the coming of Gil-galad the Elven-king in the days of the Last Alliance?

   _____

   _____

THE LORD OF THE RINGS: BOOK ONE
A Knife in the Dark, Page 2

6. Could the Black Riders see Strider and the hobbits?

_____

_____

_____

7. Who suggested building a fire and why?

_____

_____

_____

8. Where did Tinúviel rescue Beren from, and with what did Beren pay the bride-price for Lúthien?

_____

_____

_____

9. Despite Gandalf's warning, what did Frodo do as the Black Riders advanced on the hobbits?

_____

_____

10. Who did Frodo call out to as he was struck by the enemy?

_____

_____

THE LORD OF THE RINGS: BOOK ONE
Project—Weathertop Game

Supplies

game board

four Black Rider pieces

one Frodo piece

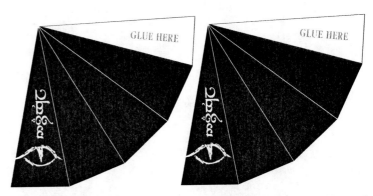

Instructions

Photocopy game pieces and game board onto card stock (copy them at 120% on 11 x 17" paper for larer pieces and a larger board). Cut out game pieces and fold, using a glue stick along the short panel and fold it under the front panel (black and white stones could be used as game pieces as well).

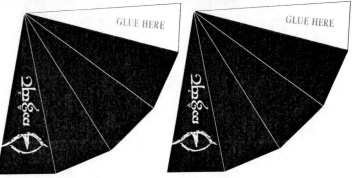

Game Play: The four Black Riders are initially placed on the dark squares at bottom edge of the board; Frodo is placed on any dark square on the top edge. The objective of Frodo is to cross from one side of the board to the other, arriving at any one of the Black Riders's original squares; the Black Riders's objective is to prevent Frodo from doing so. The Black Riders move diagonally forward one square. Frodo moves diagonally forward or backward

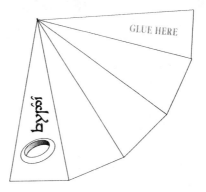

one square at a time. There is no jumping or removal of pieces. The play alternates with Frodo moving first. The player controlling the Black Riders moves only one Rider per turn. Frodo is trapped when a Black Rider occupies all four of his potential move squares. Alternatively, two Black Riders may trap Frodo against an edge of the board. There is even one corner where a single Black Rider may do the trapping. It may be noted that should a Black Rider reach Frodo's original home row, it will no longer have any potential moves.

THE LORD OF THE RINGS: BOOK ONE
Project—Sam's Troll Comic Strip

Draw each of the eight stanzas of Sam's troll poem in the spaces below.

THE LORD OF THE RINGS: BOOK ONE
Flight to the Ford

1. When the Black Rider attacked Frodo, instead of a tall, pale, crowned figure what had Sam seen?

   _____

   _____

2. What did Strider do with *Athelas* he found?

   _____

   _____

   _____

3. What did Strider find in the mud in the middle of the Last Bridge?

   _____

   _____

   _____

4. What piece of their "family history" did the hobbits come across that revived their spirits?

   _____

   _____

   _____

   _____

5. Who from the house of Elrond joined Strider and the hobbits on their journey?

_____

_____

_____

6. Who awaited the travelers at the Ford of Rivendell?

_____

_____

7. Describe what happened after Frodo rode across Ford?

_____

_____

_____

THE LORD OF THE RINGS: BOOK ONE
Project—Book Cover

This is the end of Book One, but not the end of the first book, although the author originally intended that there not be three books but one. Confused yet? It was the publisher who originally required that *The Lord of the Rings* be three books. *Imagine that the publisher has insisted that each book in the Trilogy be sold by itself. Insert a title for Book One and create an illustration for the front cover. Then write a short summary on the back cover.*

THE LORD OF THE RINGS: BOOK TWO
Many Meetings

1. What was the reason the other Black Riders were forced into the raging flood at the
    Ford of Bruinen, and what caused the waves to take the form of white riders and great
    white horses?

    _____

    _____

    _____

    _____

2. What did Pippin call Frodo on their way to the feast, and why did Gandalf chastise him?

    _____

    _____

    _____

3. Frodo saw many elves at the feast. Describe the appearance of the one the elves called
    Undómiel.

    _____

    _____

    _____

    _____

    _____

4. Whom did Frodo sit next to at the feast, and
    why was he important?

    _____

    _____

    _____

THE LORD OF THE RINGS: BOOK TWO
Many Meetings, Page 2

5. Who did Frodo get to see in the Hall of Fire?

   _____

   _____

   _____

6. What caused Frodo to perceive his old friend as a little wrinkled creature with a hungry face and bony, groping hands?

   _____

   _____

   _____

7. In Rivendell, who was called "the Dúnadan?"

   _____

8. Of what was Eärendil's ship made?

   _____

   _____

   _____

9. What did Bilbo do that made Strider think Bilbo was cheeky?

   _____

   _____

   _____

THE LORD OF THE RINGS: BOOK TWO
Project—Eärendil the Mariner

Rewrite Bilbo's poem about Eärendil the Mariner in prose.

_____

_____

_____

_____

_____

_____

_____

_____

_____

_____

_____

_____

_____

_____

_____

_____

_____

_____

_____

_____

_____

_____

THE LORD OF THE RINGS: BOOK TWO
The Council of Elrond

1. What did Gloin report concerning Balin, Ori and Oin?

   _____

   _____

   _____

2. Who was the herald of Gil-galad when Isildur cut the Ring from the hand of Sauron?

   _____

3. If not for help to defend Gondor, why did Boromir seek out Elrond?

   _____

   _____

   _____

4. What made Bilbo irate and caused him to jump to his feet to recite poetry?

   _____

   _____

   _____

5. *"It is precious to me, though I buy it with great pain."* About what was this written, who wrote it, who found it, where did they find it, and who denied the existence of a scroll that would contain such information?

   _____

   _____

   _____

   _____

   _____

   _____

THE LORD OF THE RINGS: BOOK TWO
The Council of Elrond, Page 2

6. What did the Enemy learn from Sméagol?

   _____

   _____

   _____

7. Who was unwittingly used to lure Gandalf to Orthanc?

   _____

   _____

8. Why did Gandalf say, ". . . he that breaks a
   thing to find out what it is has left the
   path of wisdom"?

   _____

   _____

   _____

9. How was Gandalf freed from the pinnacle
   of Orthanc?

   _____

   _____

   _____

   _____

10. Who gave Gandalf permission to take Shadowfax?

   _____

   _____

11. Why did the council decide that the Ring could not be given to Iarwain Ben-adar?

_____

_____

_____

12. What pleasant advice does Gandalf give to Bilbo?

_____

_____

_____

13. Why did Elrond say that Frodo was deserving of a seat among an assembly of Hador, Hurin, Turin and Beren?

_____

_____

_____

_____

THE LORD OF THE RINGS: BOOK TWO
Project—Useful Elvish Phrases

Below is a chart of elvish phrases with their phonetic pronunciations and English translations. Try your hand at some elvish and see if you can carry on some conversations with your friends.

ELVISH	PRONUNCIATION	ENGLISH
Suilaid	Soo-ih-lied	Greetings!
Im gelir ceni ad lín	Eem geh-leer keh-nee ahd leen	I am happy to see you again.
Le suilon	Lay swee-lonn	I greet thee.
Pedich Edhellen?	PEH-deekh eth-ell-ehn?	Do you speak Elvish?
Heniach nin?	Hen-ee-akh neen?	Do you understand me?
Man eneth lín?	Mahn eh-nehth leen?	What is your name?
Man carel le?	Mahn kah-rell lay?	What are you doing?
Man anírach cerin an le?	Mahn ah-NEAR-ahkh care-een ahn lay?	What can I do for you?
Le no an-uir nîn?	Lay no ahn-oo-ear neen?	Will you be mine forever?
Aníral maded?	Ah-NEAR-ahl mah-dead?	Do you want to eat?
Aníral sogad?	Ah-NEAR-ahl soe-gahd	Do you want to drink?
Sen tîr?	Sehn teer?	Is this true?
Man tolthant i 'waew?	Mahn tole-thahnt ee wye?	How is the weather?
Man sad Imladris?	Mahn sahd Eem-lahd-rees?	Where is Rivendell?
Man râd na Imladris?	Mahn rahd nah Eem-lahd-rees?	Which way to Rivendell?
Man ceril?	Mahn kare-eel?	What do you do?
Le gwennen?	Lay gwehn-nehn?	Are you married?
Man sâd telil?	Mahn sahd tehl-eel?	Where are you from?
Man mathach?	Mahn mah-thakh?	How do you feel?
Tiro!	TEAR-oh!	Look!
Gwanno ereb nin!	GWAH-no air-ehb neen!	Leave me alone!
Daro i!	DAR-oh ee!	Stop that!
Sedho!	SEH-tho!	Quiet!
Lasto!	LAHS-toe!	Listen!
No diriel!	No dear-ee-ell!	Be watchful!
Ceno!	Keh-no!	See!
Tolo hi!	Toe-loe hee!	Come now!
Avo 'osto!	Ah-voe ohs-toe!	Fear not!
Hebo estel	Heh-bo ehs-tell	Have hope.
Nostach be Orch gaer	NOST-akh bay orkh gire	You smell like ten orcs.
Dôl lost lîn	Dole lohst leen	Your head is empty.
Nai Ungoliant meditha le	Nie un-GOAL-ee-ahnt meh-DEETH-ah lay	May Ungoliant devour you.
Labo vi Orodruin	Lah-boe vee Ore-oh-DROO-inn	Go jump in Mount Doom.

ELVISH	PRONUNCIATION	ENGLISH
Ti tállbe Orch	Tee tahl-bay Orkh	Go kiss an orc!
Le hannon	Lay hah-non	Thank you.
Le melon	Lay mell-on	I love you.
Baw	Bow [rhymes with cow]	No [denying intentions].
Law	Low [as in loud]	No [denying facts].
Aur Onnad Meren!	Our oh-nahd mare-ehn!	Happy Birthday!
_____ eneth nîn	_____ eh-nehth neen	My name is _____.
Tiro na i ninniach vanui	Tear-oh nah ee neen-nee-ahkh vah-noo-ee.	Look at the beautiful rainbow.
Hû nîn mant han	Hoo neen mahnt hahn	My dog ate it.
Aníron gwanna	Ah-NEAR-on gwahn-nah	I wish I could leave.
Ae anírach	Eye ah-NEAR-ahkh	If you wish.
Gelir na thaed	Geh-leer nah thide	Happy to help.
Edro gûr lín	Eh-droe goor leen	Open your heart.
Glassen	Glahs-sehn	My pleasure.
Gurth 'ni yrch!	Goorth nee oorkh!	Death to the orcs!
Telin o Imladris	Teh-leen oh Eem-lahd-rees	I come from Rivendell.
Im maer	Eem myre.	I'm well.
Pelin pedi i lam edhellen	Peh-leen peh-dee ee lahm eh-thehl-lehn	I can speak the Elvish language.
Isusarad 'elir	Ees-oos-ahr-ahd ehl-eer	Merry Christmas!
Namárië	Nah-MAR-ee-ay	Farewell.
Garo arad vaer	GAH-roh ARE-ahd vire	Have a good day.
Noro go hûl, bado go Eru	Nore-oh go hool, BAH-doe go air-OO	Run with the wind, go with God!

THE LORD OF THE RINGS: BOOK TWO
The Ring Goes South

1. Why did Pippin think he needed to go along with the company that accompanies Frodo and the Ring?

   _____

   _____

   _____

2. Why did Elrond decide that there should be nine in the Company of the Ring?

   _____

   _____

3. What gifts did Bilbo give to Frodo?

   _____

   _____

4. Who was the only one not depressed when the Company left Rivendell?

   _____

   _____

5. What did Caradhras do to the Company?

   _____

   _____

   _____

THE LORD OF THE RINGS: BOOK TWO
A Journey in the Dark

1. Since the road to Redhorn Gate was closed to the Company, where did they decide to go instead and why did they not instead choose the Gap of Rohan?

_____

_____

_____

2. When the wolves attacked, what was the result of Gandalf crying out, *"Naur an edraith ammen! Naur dan i ngaurhoth!"*?

_____

_____

_____

3. What accounted for the lack of water flowing in the Sirannon or rushing over Stair Falls?

_____

_____

_____

4. What were the instructions wrought in *ithildin* on the Doors of Durin?

_____

5. Why did Gandalf not need the words to close the Doors?

_____

_____

6. In the *Unfinished Tales*, it is told that the Black Númenórean queen Berúthiel "had nine black cats and one white, her slaves, with whom she conversed, or read their memories, setting them to discover all the dark secrets of Gondor, . . ." According to Aragorn, who was surer of finding the way home in a blind night than these notorious felines?

_____

_____

7. What did Gandalf suggest should be thrown down a well in Moria after Pippin dropped a stone down a well in a guardroom that they came across?

_____

_____

8. On what basis did Gandalf choose their course of direction when presented with three unremembered passageways?

_____

_____

_____

9. What did Frodo learn concerning the value of his mithril corslet?

_____

_____

_____

10. Whose tomb did the Company find?

_____

_____

THE LORD OF THE RINGS: BOOK TWO
Project—The Doors of West Moria

Draw a picture below of Gandalf in front of the doors trying to enter Moria, then trace over the gray guidelines from Tolkien's illustration to complete your image.

THE LORD OF THE RINGS: BOOK TWO
The Bridge of Khazad-dûm

1. What did the Company find in the Chamber of Mazarbul, and what did it reveal about the fate of the lord of Moria?

   _____

   _____

   _____

2. What did Frodo do that made at least one cave-troll fear the Chamber of Mazarbul?

   _____

   _____

3. What did Gandalf try to do to the eastern door of the Chamber of Mazarbul?

   _____

   _____

   _____

4. What made Legolas drop an arrow and Gimli drop his axe?

   _____

   _____

5. What happened to Gandalf after he sent Durin's Bane into the abyss?

   _____

   _____

   _____

   _____

Project—From the Desk of Gimli

Pretend you are Gimli and write a letter to Glóin, reporting on what you learned about Balin in Moria and informing him about what happened on the Bridge of Khazad-dûm. Angerthas Erebor runes are shown at the bottom of the page, should you desire to write to Glóin using dwarvish lettering.

ᚠᛏᚢᛒ ᚱᚢᚺ ᚠᚺᚲᚤ ᚾᛏ ᚢᛁᛒᚷᛁ

a	b	c	d	e	f	g	h	i	j	k	l	m	n	o	p	q	r	s	t	u	v	w	x	y	z

THE LORD OF THE RINGS: BOOK TWO
Lothlórien

1. What did Gimli show Frodo in Kheled-zâram?

   _____

   _____

   _____

2. What did Aragorn discover while tending to the injuries
   of Sam and Frodo that made his heart glad?

   _____

   _____

   _____

3. Although there were no signs of Orcs chasing them, why did Frodo still think that they
   were being followed?

   _____

   _____

   _____

4. What did Legolas tell Sam soon after they had crossed the Nimrodel that caused him to
   hastily cover his own mouth?

   _____

   _____

   _____

5. Who of the Company did Haldir initially prohibit from coming into Lothlórien and
   under what conditions did he finally allow passage?

   _____

   _____

   _____

6. How did the Company cross the Celebrant?

   _____

   _____

7. How did Aragorn conciliate their stiff-necked dwarf?

   _____

   _____

8. What welcomed change occurred to the Company at Cerin Amroth?

   _____

   _____

   _____

9. Who did Frodo come across "wrapped in some fair memory" saying, *"Arwen vanimelda, namárië!"*?

   _____

   _____

THE LORD OF THE RINGS: BOOK TWO
Project—Elvish ABC's

Tolkien loved languages, even working for the Oxford English Dictionary (for which he is credited for the word *walrus*). In addition to his professional work as a philologist, he invented languages, the best known being Quenya and Sindarin, since they are at the core of his legendarium. Learning Quenya and Sindarin would be quite a task, but below is a simplified chart so you can rewrite English using Tolkien's letters. The most important thing you need to know to do this is that in the Quenya style, vowels go above/below the consonants they follow (follow the gray arrows). If a vowel begins a word, a small "carrier" mark is placed below the vowel markings. A line under a consonant indicates a double consonant. The sentence "The five boxing wizards jump quickly" might look like this:

Try writing your name using elvish lettering or translate a passage in this chapter. At the very least, learning this way of writing would be quite helpful for sending secret notes to friends!

A	↑	J		S		LD	
B		K		S		RD	
C		L		T		TH	
D		M		U	↑	CH	
E	↑	N		V		SH	
E	↓ (silent)	O	↑	W		NT	
F		P		X		ND	
G		Qu		Y	(consonant)	MP	
H		R	(as in "red")	Y	↓ (vowel)	MB	
I	↑	R	(as in "car")	Z		carrier]	
				Z			

THE LORD OF THE RINGS: BOOK TWO
The Mirror of Galadriel

1. When the Company arrived at Caras Galadhon, why were they unable to immediately enter the city?

   _____

   _____

   _____

2. What was elvish etiquette when they would meet anyone, regardless of that person's rank and status?

   _____

   _____

3. Looking deep into Sam's heart, what did the Lady Galadriel seem to offer the hobbit?

   _____

   _____

   _____

4. During their time among the Galadhrim, what unexpected companion accompanied Legolas as he went abroad in the land?

   _____

   _____

   _____

5. What did Sam want Frodo to add to his poem honoring Mithrandir?

   _____

   _____

   _____

THE LORD OF THE RINGS: BOOK TWO
The Mirror of Galadriel, Page 2

6. What did Sam see in the mirror?

_____

_____

_____

7. Who was the keeper of Nenya, the Ring of Adamant?

_____

_____

8. What test did Frodo give to Galadriel, and what was the result?

_____

_____

_____

9. What did Nenya look like to Sam?

_____

_____

_____

THE LORD OF THE RINGS: BOOK TWO
Project—Truth and Poetry

When evening in the Shire was grey
his footsteps on the Hill were heard;
before the dawn he went away
on journey long without a word.

From Wilderland to Western shore,
from northern waste to southern hill
through dragon-lair and hidden door
and darkling woods he walked at will.

With Dwarves and Hobbits, Elves and Men,
with mortal and immortal folk,
with bird on bough and beast in den,
in their own secret tongues he spoke.

A deadly sword, a healing hand,
a back that bent beneath its load;
a trumpet-voice, a burning brand,
a weary pilgrim on the road.

A lord of wisdom throned he sat,
swift in anger, quick to laugh;
an old man in a battered hat
who leaned upon a thorny staff.

He stood upon the bridge alone
and Fire and Shadow both defied;
his staff was broken on the stone,
in Khazad-dûm his wisdom died.

Sitting beside the fountain of Lórien, Frodo sets in verse his sadness at the death of Gandalf. And in Rivendell Bilbo defended Aragorn with a poem—of his own! What is it about poetry that makes something more real or validates something, making it more true? Discuss your thoughts or write a short essay in response to this idea. You might also read and discuss Dana Gioia's essay "Can Poetry Matter?" (www.danagioia.net/essays/ecpm.htm).

_____

_____

_____

_____

_____

_____

_____

_____

_____

_____

THE LORD OF THE RINGS: BOOK TWO

Project—Timeline

*How well have you been paying attention? Test
your comprehension by filling in this timeline.*

3018

APRIL

12 — Gandalf tells _____ about the Ring.

JULY

4 — _____ sets out from Minas Tirith for Rivendell.

20 — Gandalf imprisoned in Othanc by _____

SEPTEMBER

18 — Gandalf escapes from Orthanc.

19 — Gandalf comes to _____

22 — Frodo's birthday party

23 — Merry, Frodo, Sam and Pippin leave Hobbiton in two groups. | Gandalf tames _____

25 — The hobbits re-unite in _____

26 — The hobbits meet _____

28 — Hobbits captured by _____

29 — Hobbits meet Strider | Gandalf reaches Hobbiton and talks to _____

30 — Hobbits leave _____

OCTOBER

1 — Gandalf leaves Bree.

3 — Gandalf attacked on _____

6 — Hobbits and Strider attacked at night with _____ wounded.

9 — Glorfindel leaves Rivendell.

13 — Hobbits and Strider cross the _____ of Mitheithel.

18 — _____ finds Frodo at dusk. | Gandalf reaches Rivendell.

20 — Frodo escapes across the Ford of Bruinen.

24 — Frodo awakes in Rivendell and _____ arrives in Rivendell.

25 — The Council of _____

DECEMBER

25 — The Fellowship leaves Rivendell.

3019

JANUARY

11 — Company encounters _____ on Caradhras.

13 — Company reaches West Gate of _____. Gollum begins to trail.

15 — Fall of Gandalf

17 — _____ arrives at Caras Galadhon.

THE LORD OF THE RINGS: BOOK TWO
Farewell to Lórien and *The Great River*

1. What did Celeborn offer to give the Company that comforted Aragorn but troubled Sam?

   _____

   _____

2. What gifts were given to the Company as they picnicked with the Lord and Lady of Galadhrim?

   Aragorn: _____

   _____

   Boromir: _____

   _____

   Merry and Pippin: _____

   _____

   Legolas: _____

   _____

   Sam: _____

   _____

   Gimli: _____

   _____

   Frodo: _____

   _____

3. Gimli told Legolas that he would not have come on the Quest if he had known the danger. Of what danger did he speak?

   _____

   _____

   _____

THE LORD OF THE RINGS: BOOK TWO
Farewell to Lórien and *The Great River, Page 2*

4. What funny dream did Sam have, and what did he and Frodo conclude about it?

_____

_____

_____

5. What happened near Sarn Gebir—the rapids of the Great River Anduin—and why did Gimli praise the bow of Galadriel?

_____

_____

_____

6. What about the moon did Sam find puzzling, and how did Aragorn explain the apparent discrepancy?

_____

_____

_____

7. Describe Argonath—the Pillars of the Kings.

_____

_____

THE LORD OF THE RINGS: BOOK TWO
Project 1—Lembas Bread

Although one bite may not satisfy your hunger, this delicately lemon-flavored scone-type bread is a treat for Elves and Men alike.

Ingredients

3/4 cup slivered almonds

2-1/2 cups all-purpose flour

1 tbsp baking powder

1/4 tea salt

zest of 1 lemon

8 tbsps unsalted butter, cold

1/3 cup honey

1/2 cup half and half or whole milk

Directions

1. Preheat oven to 425 degrees.
2. Finely grind almonds in a food processor or blender.
3. Mix together ground almonds, flour, baking powder, salt, and zest of a lemon in a large mixing bowl.
4. Cut cold butter into small cubes and add to flour mixture.
5. Using a pastry blender or fingertips, chop butter pieces into flour mixture until mixture resembles coarse crumbs.
6. In a small bowl, whisk together honey and half and half or milk.
7. Add a small amount of milk mixture to the flour mixture and toss with a fork. Repeat until dough forms. Do not overwork dough.
8. Roll the dough out about 1/2 inch thick. Cut out 3 inches squares and transfer to an ungreased cookie sheet. Score each square from corner to corner (forming 2 triangles) with a knife. Bake for 10 to 12 minutes or until golden brown. Makes 10 to 12. Serve immediately or store in an airtight container.

THE LORD OF THE RINGS: BOOK TWO
The Breaking of the Fellowship

1. What did Sting reveal on the lawn of Parth Galen?

   _____

   _____

2. What happened while Frodo was alone that made him go sit upon the Seat of Seeing?

   _____

   _____

   _____

3. While Frodo was away, what did Aragorn decide to be the best course of action?

   _____

   _____

4. Sam disagreed with Aragorn. What did Sam say was going to happen?

   _____

   _____

5. How did Sam keep Frodo from leaving alone?

   _____

   _____

THE LORD OF THE RINGS: BOOK THREE
The Departure of Boromir and *The Riders of Rohan*

1. What did Aragorn see when he arrived at the glade about a mile from Parth Galen?

   _____

   _____

   _____

2. What did Aragorn learn—and fail to learn—concerning the fate of the hobbits?

   _____

   _____

   _____

3. Some of the dead Orcs' shields bore the mark of Saruman—what was it?

   _____

   _____

4. Instead of building a cairn, what did Gimli, Legolas and Aragorn do to honor Boromir?

   _____

   _____

   _____

5. What did Aragorn decide to do after solving the riddle of what happened to Sam, Frodo and the missing boat?

   _____

   _____

   _____

6. What did they find that assured them that they were still on the trail of the Orcs?

   _____

   _____

   _____

THE LORD OF THE RINGS: BOOK THREE
The Departure of Boromir and *The Riders of Rohan, Page 2*

7. Why did Aragorn say "Not idly do the leaves of Lorien fall," and why were they all encouraged in their pursuit?

_____

_____

_____

8. How did Aragorn describe the Riders of Rohan?

_____

_____

_____

9. Why did Gimli insult Éomer, basically saying that the Third Marshal of Riddermark's stupidity was his only excuse for his foolishness?

_____

_____

_____

10. How did Legolas respond to Éomer threatening Gimli?

_____

_____

_____

11. How did Éomer respond when he learned that Aragorn, Gimli and Legolas were looking for halflings?

_____

_____

_____

12. Why did Éomer rename Aragorn "Wingfoot?"

_____

_____

13. On what condition did Éomer permit Aragorn, Gimli and Legolas to travel through their lands and give them horses as well?

_____

_____

_____

14. What occurred during Gimli's watch the night at the edge of Fanghorn?

_____

_____

_____

_____

THE LORD OF THE RINGS: BOOK THREE
Project 1—The Book vs. the Movie

A movie is not a book and certain concessions need to be made for the medium, but not all changes are neccessary or an improvement. *After watching Peter Jackson's movie* The Fellowship of the Ring, *answer the following questions concerning variations between the books and the movie.*

1. How was Frodo's part in Bilbo's birthday party significantly changed in the movie?

   _____

   _____

2. How did the movie change the hobbits' adventures between the Shire and Bree?

   _____

   _____

   _____

   _____

   _____

   _____

   _____

   _____

   _____

   _____

3. In the movie, who replaces Glorfindel?

   _____

4. In the movie, Sam Gamgee is a peer of Frodo. What is the actual difference in their ages?

   _____

   _____

THE LORD OF THE RINGS: BOOK THREE
Project 2—Horse of Rohan

The Rohan culture was inspired by the Scandinavians and medieval Anglo-Saxons. The Riders of Rohan were famous for their horses. Beginning with the sketch below, draw a horse and then design a saddle for it that would fit with their culture.

THE LORD OF THE RINGS: BOOK THREE
The Uruk-Hai

1. What was Pippin's last memory of Boromir?

   _____

   _____

   _____

2. What were the orders given to the Orcs that kept them from simply killing the hobbits?

   _____

   _____

   _____

3. What was Pippin able to do in the aftermath of the Orcs fighting over which way they should travel?

   _____

   _____

   _____

4. What does Pippin imply to Grishnákh that encourages the Orc to take the hobbits for himself?

   _____

   _____

   _____

5. Once the Riders had the Orcs surrounded, what did the hobbits do first, before crawling towards the woods?

   _____

   _____

THE LORD OF THE RINGS: BOOK THREE
Treebeard

1. How was Fangorn not like Bilbo's description of Mirkwood but instead reminiscent of the old room in the Great Place of the Tooks in the Smials at Tuckborough?

   _____

   _____

   _____

   _____

2. Describe the person the hobbits met after they had climbed and scrambled to the top of the *a-lalla-lalla-rumba-kamanda-lind-or-burúmë*.

   _____

   _____

   _____

   _____

   _____

3. What was the vocation of Ents?

   _____

   _____

THE LORD OF THE RINGS: BOOK THREE
Treebeard

4. What was the effect on the hobbits of the drinks they had at the ent-house?

_____

_____

_____

5. Why were the hobbits asked to describe the Shire and its country over and over again?

_____

_____

_____

6. Who is described as having "a mind of metal and wheels" who "does not care for growing things" and who was always willing to listen but never repaid in kind?

_____

_____

7. What happened to the Entwives?

_____

_____

_____

_____

_____

8. How did Bregalad get his nickname?

_____

_____

_____

9. What was it that the Orcs had done that so roused the Ents?

_____

_____

THE LORD OF THE RINGS: BOOK THREE
Project—Tree Shepherd

After reading the following information on trees, go outside for a nature walk. See if you can discover the "story" behind the trees you come across. Then consider planting a tree yourself so you can shepherd it yourself.

The character of Treebeard recurs frequently in *The Lord of the Rings*. He is an Ent, a self-described "tree shepherd;" it is his life's work to tend to the trees in his forest. As a tree shepherd he can speak to the trees and inquire as to their health and well being. We, however, are not Ents or tree shepherds; we must devise other ways of listening to what trees have to tell us.

Fortunately, there are many ways that trees show their general health by their appearance, several of which are easily seen with just a little bit of observation.

Trees exist both above and below the surface of the soil; the roots below the soil are vital to the nutrition and support of the rest of the tree. Roots are found mostly in the top three feet of soil and most of those are found in the top 12 inches. So the idea that a tree's roots are a mirror image of its branches is a myth. The roots extend out to around three times as far as the branches (an important reason to plant large trees far away from buildings and other structures). When the roots are damaged it affects the rest of the tree. In fact, a root on a particular side of a tree generally corresponds with a branch on the same side of the tree. So, if a major root on the left side of a tree is damaged, you can expect the branch on the left side of the tree associated with that root to suffer or die.

This leads us to branches. They are generally responsible for themselves because there is little sharing of nutrients among branches. This is one of the reasons an otherwise healthy tree can have dead or dying branches interspersed throughout the healthy ones.

You may have noticed that the place where a branch inserts into the trunk has a kind of knobby ring around it. This is called a branch collar and is a sign that the branch is firmly attached to the tree and is likely very strong. Branches have a kind of woody core that goes into the trunk of the tree and grows deeper and stronger as time passes. The growth rings of the branch interweave with the growth rings of the trunk to form a strong bond. You can see the evidence of these woody cores in lumber in the form of knots in the wood.

When branches do not form a bark collar, they are called "suckers". These branches form low down on the trunk below the level of older, stronger branches, or they grow from the stump of a tree that has been cut down. Suckers do not form a strong bond with the trunk. They do not insert their woody core into the trunk and are, therefore, structurally unsound.

Tree trunks are the columns that support the branches of the tree. Most trunks are single and then gradually divide into a crown of branches. Sometimes, however, they split and grow into two competing trunks that form either a "U" shape or "V" shape. If the two trunks form a "U" (or a "crotch" as it is sometimes called) where bark can be seen clearly, this is safe for the tree and structurally sound. However, if the two trunks form a "V" where the bark disappears into a dark crevice, this could mean trouble for the tree in the future. Water and dirt accumulate in these crevices and foster disease and rot which are obviously bad for the tree. But a more subtle danger to the tree comes as the two trunks grow; both of

Project—Tree Shepherd, Page 2

them will continue to increase in girth, thereby forcing the trunks apart and forming a split at the base of the trunk. At least one side of the tree will end up falling when the stress grows too great for the trunks to remain joined (this is bad if the side that falls is facing your house!).

Trees can also indicate that the land on which they are growing has been moving. Rock and soil will slowly move down a slope over time; geologists refer to this process as "downhill creep." Trees that have been growing on a hill can show evidence of creep by the shape of their trunks. Trees, as a rule, grow straight up; when trees on a hillside seem to grow out at an angle and then slowly curve up, this shows that the upper layers of the soil are moving downhill (and taking the trees with them).

Before planting a tree, read the selection below and utilize the abundant resources available at local nurseries.

Choosing a Tree

Choose a tree that is specifically hardy and native to your area. Be aware of localized areas where weather conditions might differ from the norm (a north-facing slope or sheltered yard). Consider the size of the full-grown tree and its life expectancy. A small tree planted today might grown into an over-sized tree to be removed in a few years. Take a look around your neighborhood and avoid planting a tree that is already present in over-abundance. Many trees are purchased for their ornamental value such as leaf color, flower or fruit. Many fruiting trees attract wildlife which may not be desired for all. Think about where the tree is to be planted and find a tree that will thrive in the location you

have chosen without being too close to buildings or casting shade on your vegetable garden.

Planting the Tree

Late summer or early fall is the best time to plant new trees in many areas. This gives the new tree time to establish its roots before winter arrives and the ground freezes. Trees can also be planted in late winter or early spring, but avoid planting in the hot summer weather. Before digging, identify the location of any underground utilities, then follow the planting instructions which come with your tree. Remember that root tips dry easily when exposed to air, so work quickly once the tree is removed from the pot. Water thoroughly after planting, then mulch a three-foot diameter circle around the base of the tree. Depending on the size of the tree, staking may be needed for extra support.

Maintenance

For the first few years, watch your tree closely for signs of moisture stress. This can be seen in leaf wilting or hard, caked soil. Water trees slowly, allowing the water to soak in which will encourage deep root growth. Fertilizers are not usually needed for newly planted trees but may be used later as the tree grows. Pruning is also not necessary for newly planted trees, but as limbs grown pruning will become necessary. Low branches, suckers (see "Tree Shepherd" project), and dead or damaged limbs should be removed. Young trees do need to be protected against rodents, frost, cracks, sunscald and lawn equipment.

THE LORD OF THE RINGS: BOOK THREE
The White Rider

1. Why did Aragorn think that it wasn't Saruman who scared off their horses?

   _____

   _____

2. What clue led Aragorn to deduce that at least one of the hobbits was still alive?

   _____

   _____

3. Where did Gimli, Legolas and Aragorn reunite with Gandalf, and in what way was he now Saruman?

   _____

   _____

   _____

4. How could it be true what Gandalf said that Boromir "escaped in the end"?

   _____

   _____

   _____

5. According to Gandalf, why do old people talk to themselves?

   _____

   _____

   _____

6. What did Sauron imagine was the strategy of the Company, and what course of action had not even crossed his mind, thereby giving them hope?

_____

_____

_____

7. According to Gandalf, about what danger, close at hand, had Saruman forgotten?

_____

_____

8. How did the balrog and Gandalf get from below the deepest delvings of the dwarves in Moria to Durin's Tower at the summit of Celebdil for the Battle of the Peak?

_____

_____

_____

9. When Legolas and Aragorn received words from Galadriel about the Dead and dying, why was Gimli so happy that he sang and did a little jig?

_____

_____

_____

10. What could be deduced about Merry and Pippin from the smoke Legolas saw through the Gap of Rohan?

_____

_____

_____

THE LORD OF THE RINGS: BOOK THREE
The King of the Golden Hall

1. What did the Doorward of Théoden require of Gandalf and his companions, and what was the only thing that Háma did not get?

   _____

   _____

2. What did Wormtongue name "Master Stormcrow"?

   _____

   _____

3. What did Gandalf do to Gríma after the son of Gálmód insulted Galadriel?

   _____

   _____

4. Where did Háma find Herugrim (along with many other things that had been missing)?

   _____

   _____

5. What did Gandalf surmise was the price with which Saruman bought Gríma's service?

   _____

   _____

   _____

6. What merciful choice did Théoden give to Wormtongue?

   _____

   _____

   _____

7. Who did Théoden leave in charge as he set off to war?

   _____

   _____

THE LORD OF THE RINGS: BOOK THREE
Project—Felaróf Tapestry

At the foot of the White Mountains in the town of Edoras, atop a high platform, built upon a green terrace on a hill, stood the great hall Meduseld. Its thatched roof gleamed golden in the sunlight and images of beasts and birds with jewelled eyes and golden claws cavorted on its northern doors. Inside the long main room of Meduseld on the walls were woven cloths depicting the history of the Rohirrim, including that of Eorl the Young mounted on Felaróf. Ancestor of the *mearas*—the great horses of Rohan— Felaróf was a beautiful white horse, said to be from a line of horses whose sire was brought to Middle-earth from the Undying Lands. In 2510, Eorl rode Felaróf to the aid of Gondor at the Battle of the Field of Celebrant.

Color this tapestry of Shadowfax's famous ancestor.

THE LORD OF THE RINGS: BOOK THREE
Helm's Deep

1. Before Gandalf and Shadowfax left for a "swift errand," what instruction did the White Rider give to Théoden?

   _____

   _____

   _____

2. How were Gúthwinë and Andúril able to surprise the rammers at the Hornburg-gate?

   _____

   _____

   _____

3. What happened that gave Éomer reason to comment that "oft the unbidden guest proves the best company"?

   _____

   _____

   _____

4. After Orcs crept through the drain under Deeping Wall, how high did Gimli's *tale* (an archaic word meaning "count") of hewn foes reach?

   _____

   _____

THE LORD OF THE RINGS: BOOK THREE
Helm's Deep, Page 2

5. What happened as Aragorn cited the lore that Hornburg had never been taken by a foe if men defended it?

_____

_____

_____

6. What happened at dawn as the Deep echoed with horn blasts?

_____

_____

_____

7. What terrified the Orcs, sending them wailing under the shadow of the trees—from which they never returned?

_____

_____

_____

THE LORD OF THE RINGS: BOOK THREE
Project—Helm's Deep Map

From the description in the book, try to label the map below to include: the Hornburg (the great tower on which rested the great horn of Helm Hammerhand), the Deeping Wall, the postern door, Great Gate, Outer Court, Inner Court, and the Rear Gate. Also draw arrows in the direction in which lie the series of hills called Helm's Dike and the Glittering Caves.

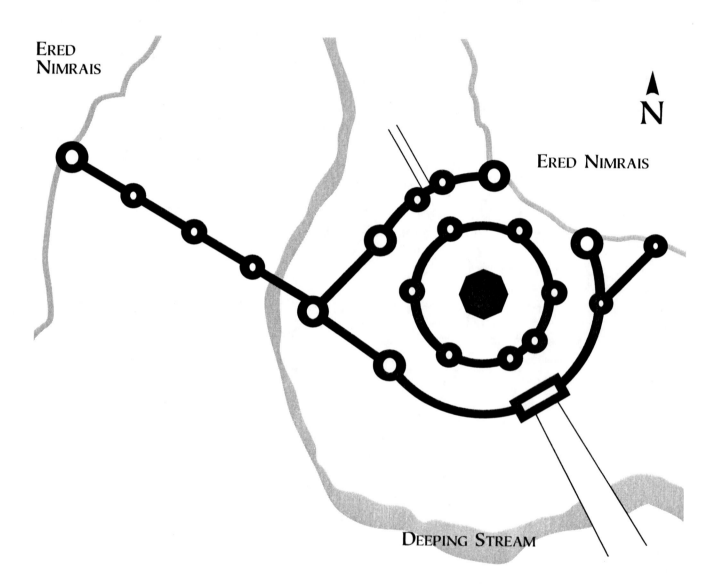

ERED NIMRAIS

N

ERED NIMRAIS

DEEPING STREAM

THE LORD OF THE RINGS: BOOK THREE
The Road to Isengard

1. What was the tally in Legolas and Gimli's game when they reunited that morning?

   _____

   _____

2. What "wizardry" was credited to Gandalf for which he claimed to have had no part?

   _____

   _____

   _____

3. Erkenbrand ordered the men of Dunland to help repair what was broken in the battle, take an oath to never pass the Fords of Isen armed, and promise not to march with the enemies of men. Why did this decree amaze the hillmen?

   _____

   _____

   _____

   _____

4. Following Gimli's rhapsodic description of the Caverns of Helm's Deep, what bargain did the elf and dwarf make?

   _____

   _____

   _____

5. When the company of riders left the forest, what did Legolas see in the woods and what stuff of legend did Théoden encounter?

   _____

   _____

   _____

6. What was the Death Down and how was it made?

_____

_____

_____

_____

7. Describe Isengard.

_____

_____

_____

_____

_____

_____

_____

_____

_____

_____

_____

_____

8. Who were the doorwardens of Isengard, and how were they occupied when Gandalf and company arrived?

_____

_____

_____

9. What "danger" from Merry did Gandalf spare Théoden?

_____

_____

10. Who was guarding Orthanc while most of the Ents were getting clean water to drink?

_____

_____

_____

THE LORD OF THE RINGS: BOOK THREE
Flotsam and Jetsam

1. As Gimli, Aragorn, Legolas and the hobbits sat down to eat (or eat again, as in the case of the hobbits), what did Gimli notice that Legolas believed could be credited to the draughts of Fanghorn?

   _____

   _____

   _____

2. What treasure ("as precious as the Ring to me") does Pippin part with that places Gimli in debt to the halfling?

   _____

   _____

3. How many days had passed since the hobbits had been taken?

   _____

4. What items did Aragorn return to the hobbits? And according to Merry's report, what effect had some of these items had on Uglúk, the captain of Saruman's Uruk-hai?

   _____

   _____

   _____

5. What did Merry think Huorns were?

   _____

   _____

   _____

6. What happened to the Ent named Beechbone?

   _____

   _____

THE LORD OF THE RINGS: BOOK THREE
Flotsam and Jetsam, Page 2

7. When Gandalf and the hobbits were initially reunited, what greeting did the White Rider make to Pippin?

_____

_____

8. What did Treebeard and the other Ents do that so pleased Treebeard, and what was the effect of their labors on Isengard?

_____

_____

_____

_____

9. "Put all the rats in one trap," Gandalf had told Treebeard. Who was directly impacted by Treebeard's execution of this assignment?

_____

_____

_____

10. After hearing Merry and Pippin's accountings, what small matter puzzled Aragorn?

_____

_____

_____

_____

THE LORD OF THE RINGS: BOOK THREE
Project—Heroic Poem

A heroic couplet is made from a sequence of rhyming pairs of iambic pentameter lines. A line of iambic pentameter sounds like this: *da DUM da DUM da DUM da DUM da DUM.* Following is an example of heroic couplets from *Cooper's Hill* by John Denham, describing the Thames:

> O could I flow like thee, and make thy stream
> My great example, as it is my theme!
> Though deep, yet clear, though gentle, yet not dull,
> Strong without rage, without o'erflowing full.

And here is an example by William Shakespeare from his *Sonnet XVIII*:

> Shall I compare thee to a summer's day?
> Thou art more lovely and more temperate:
> Rough winds do shake the darling buds of May.
> And summer's leashe hath all too short a date:

Write a poem about the Ents's battle at Isengard in the form of a heroic couplet. Try to write at least three verses. You might want to devote one verse to the March, one to the battle (perhaps mentioning the fall of Beechbone) and one about the end of the battle.

THE LORD OF THE RINGS: BOOK THREE
The Voice of Saruman and *The Palantír*

1. Of all the things Saruman could do to his visitors, what did Gandalf warn them about?

   _____

   _____

2. Under what conditions did Théoden say that he would be at peace with Saruman?

   _____

   _____

   _____

3. What did Gandalf suggest was the career track that Saruman *should* have taken in life?

   _____

   _____

   _____

4. What did Gandalf offer to Saruman as conditions for his freedom?

   _____

   _____

   _____

5. After casting Saruman out of the Council, what did Gandalf break before Wormtongue hurled a seeing stone out of the window?

   _____

   _____

6. What did Legolas ask of Treebeard that was almost too much for the Master of Fanghorn's Wood?

   _____

   _____

   _____

7. For what did Gandalf have to forgive Pippin?

_____

_____

_____

8. Who was given charge of the palantír of Orthanc?

_____

_____

9. If the palantíri were not made by Saruman or Sauron, where did they come from?

_____

_____

_____

10. Pippin thought Gandalf was headed to Helm's Deep. But instead, at the end of this chapter, where were Gandalf and Pippin riding?

_____

_____

THE LORD OF THE RINGS: BOOK FOUR
The Taming of Sméagol and *The Passage of the Marshes*

1. What change from lembas did Sam long for?

   _____

   _____

2. Though he may be "nowt but a ninnyhammer," what was Sam able to offer to Frodo that Frodo was able to see following the fly-by by the nazgûl?

   _____

   _____

3. Though they escaped from the Emyn Muil, it appeared that they had to sacrifice a product of the Elf-country to do so. What unexpectedly happened to relieve them of that loss, and to what did Sam and Frodo each credit it?

   _____

   _____

   _____

   _____

4. What stopped Frodo from killing Gollum outright when they caught him at the broken feet of the Emyn Muil?

   _____

   _____

5. What did Frodo make Gollum swear in order to be freed of the elvish rope?

   _____

   _____

   _____

THE LORD OF THE RINGS: BOOK FOUR
Sméagol and Marshes, Page 2

6. What is *"Alive without breath; as cold as death; never thirsting, ever drinking; clad in mail, never clinking"*?

   _____

   _____

7. Why did Sméagol not eat with the hobbits?

   _____

   _____

   _____

8. Why was Frodo not terribly concerned with rationing their food?

   _____

   _____

   _____

9. What did Sam learn about the Dead Marshes by tripping?

   _____

   _____

   _____

   _____

10 What happened that frightened them all and that Sam marked as a turning point in Gollum's behavior?

   _____

   _____

   _____

   _____

THE LORD OF THE RINGS: BOOK FOUR
Sméagol and *Marshes, Page 3*

11. What loophole in his promise did Gollum suggest to Sméagol that would enable them to be as "good as fish, sweet one, but to ourselfs"?

_____

_____

_____

12. What decadent delicacy did Gollum imagine having, once he was "Lord Sméagol?"

_____

_____

_____

THE LORD OF THE RINGS: BOOK FOUR
Project—Dead Marshes Maze

The Dead Marshes were a maze of pools, mires, and waterways where a great battle had been fought during the War of the Last Alliance. The air in that region was thick with stinking mists and faces of the dead could still be seen in the wide pools in the middle of the marshes. In *The Letters of J. R. R. Tolkien,* Tolkien speculated that his description of the Dead Marshes may have been based on his personal experience in World War I, specifically, the Battle of the Somme. *Find your way through the Dead Marshes maze.*

The Lord of the Rings: Book Four
Project—Stinker Sock Sméagol

Supplies

one pair of Rockford Red Heel Socks
(Fox River Mills)

stuffing (cut up nylon stockings,
shredded foam rubber, etc.)

two large, pale buttons

scissors

pen

needle

pin

thread

> WHAT DOES HE HAVE IN HIS **SOCKSSSS**, MY PRECIOUS?

Directions

Turn the socks inside out.

Find the center of the sock and draw a line down the middle from approximately 1 1/2" below the heel to the opening. Sew a seam 1/2" away from the center line, down toward the bottom, curving the seam at the bottom to make the feet. Repeat for the other leg, remembering to leave space between the legs for stuffing.

Turn sock right side out, so the seams are on the inside. Stuff the head, body and legs. Whip stitch the opening closed.

Cut out the white and red heel area of the second sock, leaving a 1/2" area of brown around the cut out. Turn under these brown edges, center, position, and fasten lower area of mouth with pins to the body. Whip stitch the bottom of the mouth onto

the body and stuff. Then stitch the rest of the mouth to the body. Sew on the buttons for eyes just above the mouth.

Sew a 1/4" seam around rounded sides of ears. Turn right side out and stuff lightly. Turn under 1/4" at opening and whip stitch ears to the body.

Cut out the white toe area of the second sock, leaving about 3/4" area of brown around the cut out. Make two small cuts in the tip, as shown, to complete the shorts. Slip the legs through these cuts and slide up.

Cut the remaining area above the heel of the second sock into two rectangles for the arms. Fold the rectangles in half the long way, with right sides together. From the brown ends stitch 1/4" seams down the long sides of the rectangle, curving the seam at the bottom to make the rounded hands. Turn right side out, then stuff. Center the arms, turn under 1/4" around the opening and whip stitch the arms to the body.

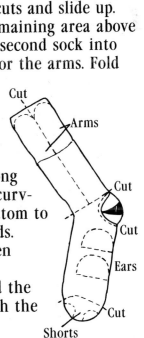

THE LORD OF THE RINGS: BOOK FOUR
The Black Gate is Closed and *Of Herbs and Stewed Rabbit*

1. Ironically, who built the Teeth of Mordor for Sauron?

   _____

   _____

2. What did Sméagol suggest that Frodo do, instead of letting Sauron have it?

   _____

   _____

3. Frodo warned Sméagol of the danger he was in if Sméagol didn't remain true to his promise made on the Ring. What did Frodo say he would do to Sméagol in a worse-case scenario?

   _____

   _____

   _____

   _____

4. Sauron was not worried about an attack from the west. Who guarded the Tower of Cirith Ungol?

   _____

   _____

   _____

5. What food did Sméagol find for the hobbits—after Sams asked nicely?

   _____

   _____

   _____

THE LORD OF THE RINGS: BOOK FOUR
The Black Gate is Closed and *Of Herbs and Stewed Rabbit*

6. What did Sam do with Sméagol's findings that so vexed the Slinker and Stinker?

_____

_____

_____

7. What relation to the High Warden of the White Tower did Sam and Frodo meet?

_____

_____

_____

8. How did the Haradrim outfit their mûmakil for battle?

_____

_____

_____

_____

_____

_____

THE LORD OF THE RINGS: BOOK FOUR
Project—Rabbit Stew

Back in the Shire, Sam would have included onions, carrots, taters and used a nice hearty broth to make his stew, but in Ithilien, he went without. You could also omit these items, using water instead of chicken broth for a more authentic taste.

Ingredients

1/4 cup vegetable oil

1 lb rabbit (or chicken) cut-up into bite-size pieces

1 medium onion, diced

2 large carrots, peeled and diced

2 medium potatoes, scrubbed and diced

2 bay leaves

5 cups chicken broth

1/2 tsp coarse salt

1/4 tsp black pepper

1 tbsp chopped fresh thyme

1 1/2 tsp chopped fresh sage

Directions

In a large, heavy-bottomed pot, heat oil over medium-high heat. Add meat pieces and brown on all sides. Remove meat with a slotted spoon and set aside. Reduce heat to medium and add onion. Sauté for 5-6 minutes or until just soft. Add carrots and potatoes and cook 3-4 minutes more, stirring often. Add meat back into pot along with chicken stock, bay leaf, salt and pepper. Bring to a boil, reduce heat and simmer for 45 minutes or until meat is tender. Add fresh herbs during the last few minutes of cooking.
Yields 5-6 servings.

THE LORD OF THE RINGS: BOOK FOUR
The Window on the West

1. To what did Faramir's interogation of Frodo keep returning?

_____

_____

2. What sad news did Frodo learn before Sam jumped in and challenged Faramir's "sauce"?

_____

_____

3. When discussing his knowledge and study in ancient lore, Faramir mentioned a pilgrim who sometimes taught him—once known as Olórin. To whom was he referring?

_____

_____

4. Under what circumstances did Faramir say that he would be willing to take up the weapon of the Dark Lord?

_____

_____

_____

5. What custom did Faramir and his men have before eating their meals?

_____

_____

_____

6. How did Frodo retell the adventures of the Company for the benefit of his host?

_____

_____

_____

7. Faramir described the decay of Gondor. To what did he attribute their decline?

_____

_____

_____

_____

8. Who was like a great tree in flower, hard as diamonds, soft as moonlight, warm as sunlight and cold as frost in the stars?

_____

_____

9. How did Sam open his big mouth—and stick his foot into it—in regards to Faramir?

_____

_____

_____

10. What compliment did Sam give to Faramir as the captain laid Frodo down to sleep?

_____

_____

THE LORD OF THE RINGS: BOOK FOUR
The Forbidden Pool and *Journey to the Cross-Roads*

1. Why did Frodo have to be "tricksy" and "false" to Sméagol?

   _____

   _____

   _____

2. Why did Faramir counsel Frodo to not follow Sméagol into the passes above Minas Morgul—the Tower of Black Sorcery?

   _____

   _____

   _____

   _____

3. What did Faramir give to the hobbits as a parting gift?

   _____

   _____

   _____

4. What had the maggot-folk of Mordor done to an old statue of one of the kings of Argonath that Frodo and Sam came across?

   _____

   _____

   _____

5. As a ray of light unexpectedly broke through the darkness, what did the hobbits see there that inspired them?

   _____

   _____

   _____

LORD OF THE RINGS
Project—Ancient King of Gondor

Recreate the defaced statue of an ancient King of Gondor.

Supplies

drawing of king *(on the following page)*

empty half-gallon orange juice carton

newspaper

bucket

large spoon

5 1/2 cups water

7 cups plaster of Paris

3 cups vermiculite

dull dinner knife for carving

coarse and fine sandpaper

glaze *(optional)*

wreath of flowers

Directions

1. Enlarge the statue art on the following page by photocopying at 125% on legal (8-1/2 x 14 inch) paper.
2. Cut the top off of a half-gallon carton and place it on newspaper.
3. In bucket, add water. Slowly stir in plaster with spoon and then vermiculite.
4. Quickly fill the carton with the plaster mixture. Carefully tap the mixture down a few times to release air bubbles.
5. After one hour, tear away the carton. Leave the plaster to harden for a few hours. When you begin carving, the plaster block should still be a bit soft.
6. Fold the enlarged photocopy of the king to the outside of the plaster block. Tape into place.
7. Using a sharp pencil, trace over the lines of the drawing. Press hard enough so that lines show on the plaster. Take off the paper.
8. Imagine the three-dimensional shape you are carving. Using kitchen knife, begin carving away the plaster *outside* the lines. As the marks on the plaster begin to be carved away, refer to the original drawing to guide you.
9. Carve the largest areas before moving on to more detailed areas.
10. After carving, smooth the sculpture by first sanding with coarse sandpaper and finishing with fine sandpaper.
11. Clean off the dust and allow to harden completely for about a week.
12. *Optional:* Glaze with mixture of equal parts water and white glue. Adorn the king with a garland of flowers like honeysuckle, morning glory, or bindweed.

THE LORD OF THE RINGS: BOOK FOUR
The Stairs of Cirith Ungol and *Shelob's Lair*

1. What was Frodo tempted to do at the pale bridge into Minas Morgul?

   _____

   _____

2. When the Lord of the Nine Riders stopped near them at the entrance of the bridge, what was Frodo able to grasp instead of the Ring that urgently commanded him?

   _____

   _____

3. What followed the Straight Stair?

   _____

   _____

4. ". . . [T]he great tales never end . . ." How were Sam and Frodo part of the great tale of Beren getting the Silmaril from the Iron Crown in Thangorodrim?

   _____

   _____

   _____

5. When the hobbits imagined the retelling of the story of brave Frodo and Samwise the Stouthearted, what did Sam try to ask Gollum?

   _____

   _____

   _____

6. When Gollum eventually returned, what did he tell Sam that he was doing?

   _____

   _____

THE LORD OF THE RINGS: BOOK FOUR
The Stairs of Cirith Ungol and *Shelob's Lair, Page 2*

7. What did Sam declare that the elves would make a song of, if they heard of Sam and Frodo's trip into Torech Ungol?

_____

_____

_____

8. What "dainties" was Sauron willing to share with the last child of Ungoliant?

_____

_____

_____

9. How did Sam's staff get broken?

_____

_____

_____

_____

_____

_____

THE LORD OF THE RINGS: BOOK FOUR
The Choices of Master Samwise

1. Why was Sam able to use Sting against Shelob and Frodo was not?

   _____

   _____

2. How did Shelob help Sam wound her worse than ever could the doughtiest soldier of old Gondor or the most savage Orc?

   _____

   _____

   _____

3. What was the final thing that Sam did that sent Shelob reeling away in defeat?

   _____

   _____

   _____

4. What did Sam take—and not take—from Frodo?

   _____

   _____

   _____

5. Though he wasn't given courage, what did Sam suddenly have the ability to do?

   _____

   _____

   _____

6. What did Sam learn about Frodo from Shagrat?

   _____

   _____

   _____

THE LORD OF THE RINGS: BOOK FOUR
The Choices of Master Samwise, Page 2

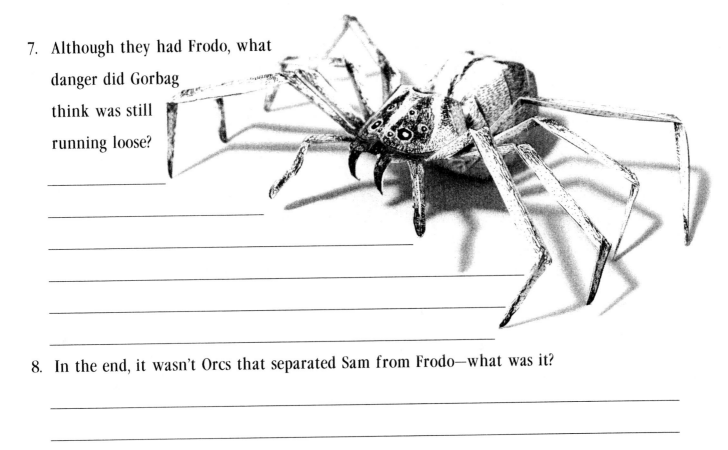

7. Although they had Frodo, what danger did Gorbag think was still running loose?

_____

_____

_____

_____

_____

_____

8. In the end, it wasn't Orcs that separated Sam from Frodo—what was it?

_____

_____

THE LORD OF THE RINGS: BOOK FOUR
Project—Shelob Paper Model

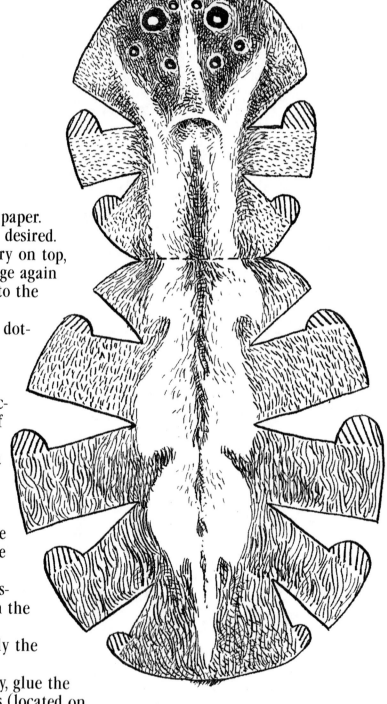

Supplies

scissors

paper (heavy cardstock)

glue

Instructions

1. Photocopy the artwork onto heavy paper.
2. Color or paint the terrible spider as desired. *Note:* If you want the legs to be hairy on top, sketch in hairs or photocopy the page again on regular copy paper and glue on to the top of the legs.
3. Cut out along bold lines. Fold along dotted lines.
4. Beginning with Shelob's disgusting head and back, glue the flaps with parallel diagonal lines under the section of the body directly in front of them. Once all tabs are glued, the result should be like a cup or half a nut shell.
5. Move on to her prickly legs and revolting abdomen on the second cut out. For best results, lightly score the legs lengthwise down the middle and on the reverse side to facilitate folding. Fold as indicated in the illustration of the completed monster on the previous page.
6. Glue flaps on the abdomen in exactly the same manner as in step 4.
7. When both pieces are completely dry, glue the remaining tabs with diagonal stripes (located on abdomen and between fangs) to the inside of the top of the spider.
8. Cajole and wrangle Shelob to fold her terrifying legs and bulging abdomen in the exact manner you would like.

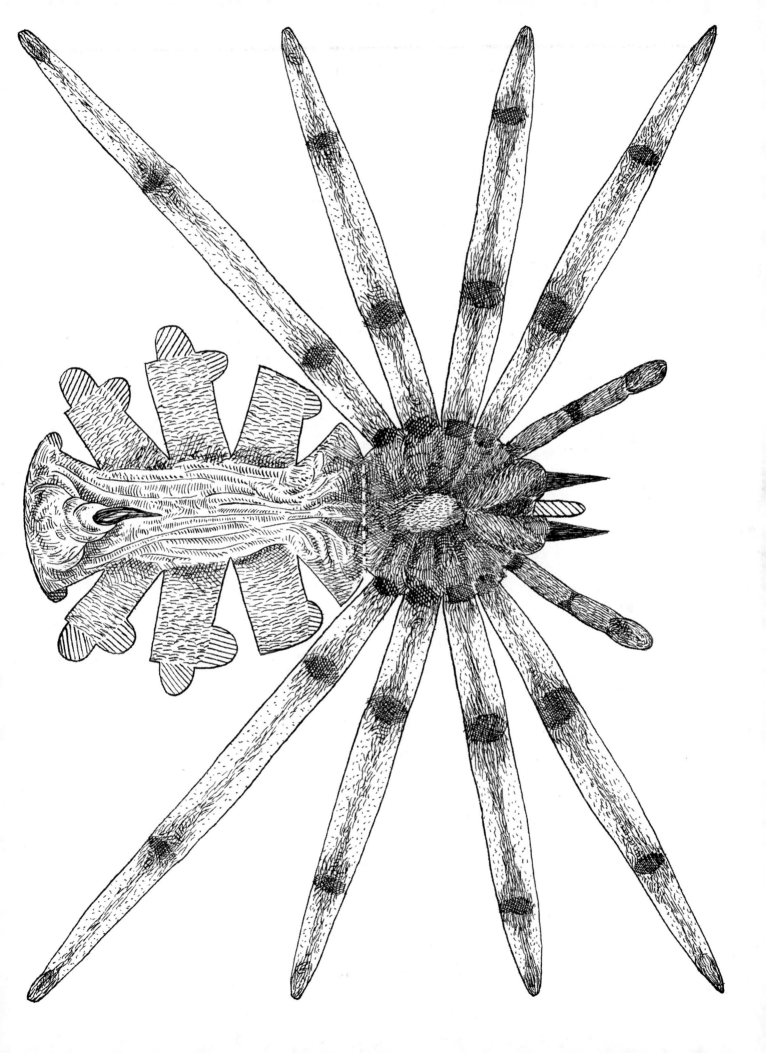

THE LORD OF THE RINGS: BOOK FOUR
Project—The Book vs. the Movie

Tolkien considered Orthanc and Minas Morgul as being the two towers from the book's title, but in Jackson's movie they are instead Orthanc and Barad-dûr. *After watching Peter Jackson's movie* The Two Towers, *answer the following questions concerning differences between the book and the movie.*

1. In the movie, Faramir talks about taking the Ring from Frodo, but in the book what is Faramir's attitude toward the Ring?

    _____

    _____

    _____

2. In the movie, Faramir takes Frodo, Sam and Gollum to Osgiliath, but in the book how far does he take them before letting them go?

    _____

    _____

3. What complete fabrication in the movie happens to Aragorn on the way to Helm's Deep to keep the Arwen/Aragorn love interest alive?

    _____

    _____

    _____

    _____

4. In the movie Elrond sends Arwen to the West—what happens that makes her decide to return to Rivendell?

    _____

    _____

    _____

THE LORD OF THE RINGS: BOOK FOUR
Project—The Book vs. the Movie, Page 2

5. Where does Old Man Willow finally appear in the movie, and who stands in for Tom Bombadil in that scene?

_____

_____

_____

6. Instead of a deliberate decision at an entmoot, in the movie why does Treebeard decide to attack Isengard?

_____

_____

_____

THE LORD OF THE RINGS: BOOK FIVE
Minas Tirith

1. On the third day of riding with Gandalf, what did Pippin see that he took for dragons?

   _____

   _____

2. Describe what distinguishing feature—part primeval shaping, part a mighty labor of old —divided Minas Tirith in two.

   _____

   _____

   _____

   _____

3. Why did Gandalf warn Pippin to watch what he said to the Lord and Steward of Minas Tirith and why, particularly, not to mention Strider?

   _____

   _____

   _____

4. Who would Denethor have wished to have died instead of Boromir?

   _____

   _____

   _____

5. What did Pippin offer to Denethor in payment of his debt to Boromir?

   _____

   _____

   _____

6. What did Gandalf say that Denethor was able to glean from their hour interview, and why was Gandalf insulted by the interview?

_____

_____

_____

7. Who did Pippin meet at nine that morning, and what burning question did he ask?

_____

_____

_____

8. What was Osgiliath, and who drove back the enemy earlier that year so that the men of Gondor still held the western half of it?

_____

_____

_____

_____

9. Who was with *Ernil i Pheriannath* at the arrival of Forlong the Fat?

_____

_____

10. Why did Gandalf say that he would not take Pippin to Denethor at sunrise, although sunrise was when the halfling was supposed to be summoned?

_____

_____

_____

_____

LORD OF THE RINGS
Project—Minas Tirith

From your reading of the chapter, try to identify each part of Minas Tirith by placing letters from the diagrams by each item on the following list.

___1. Embrasure

___2. White Tree

___3. Fen Hollen

___4. Great Gate

___5. The Hallows

___6. King's House

___7. Old Guesthouse

___8. Mount Mindolluin

___9. House of Healing

___10. Othram (City Wall)

___11. House of the Stewards

___12. Rath Dinen (Silent Street)

___13. House of the Kings

___14. Place of the Fountain

___15. White Tower of Ecthelion

___16. Gandalf and Pippen's Room

___17. Merethrond (Great Hall of Feast)

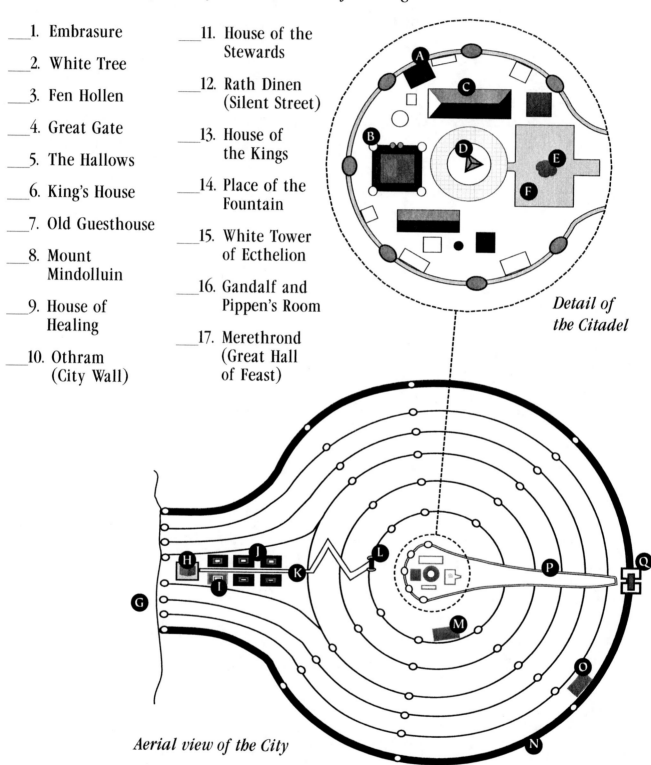

Detail of the Citadel

Aerial view of the City

THE LORD OF THE RINGS: BOOK FIVE
The Passing of the Grey Company

1. Just after the departure of Gandalf on March 5th, Aragorn, Legolas, Gimli and Merry began traveling with the riders of Rohan. They were unexpectedly joined by whom?

_____

_____

2. What message did Elrohir bring to Aragorn from Elrond?

_____

_____

_____

3. Who did Théoden choose to serve him as his esquire?

_____

_____

4. What grimmer struggle than the battle of Helm's Deep did Aragorn make and what change of course did he choose in the wake of it?

_____

_____

_____

5. What curse did Isildur place on the Men of the Mountain at the Stone of Erech?

_____

_____

_____

6. Although she extended hospitality and welcome to all, upon whom did Lady Éowyn's eyes rest most of all?

_____

7. What did Lady Éowyn say was the only thing she feared?

_____

_____

8. At the Dark Door, who was the last of Aragorn's company that entered and the one who was ever hindmost?

_____

_____

9. What did Aragorn require of the Oathbreakers to fulfill their oath and have peace?

_____

_____

_____

_____

10. What device was seen on the standard that Aragorn bade Halbarad to unfurl?

_____

_____

THE LORD OF THE RINGS: BOOK FIVE
The Muster of Rohan

1. As they arrived at Harrowdale, what counsel did Éomer give to Théoden?

   _____

   _____

2. Where did Merry see the Púkel-men, and what did they look like?

   _____

   _____

   _____

3. When and why did Baldor, son of Brego, pass into the Paths of the Dead?

   _____

   _____

   _____

4. What did Hirgon, the messenger from Gondor, present to Théoden?

   _____

   _____

5. On March 10th Merry saw a darkness coming out of the east, as did Aragorn as he led the Shadow Host from Erech, as did Pippin from the walls of Minas Tirith, as did Frodo, Sam and Gollum at Minas Morgul. What did Théoden do on the Dawnless Day that made Merry so unhappy?

   _____

   _____

   _____

6. _"Where will wants not, a way opens."_ What name did the lithe rider give after offering to take Merry along with the Lord of the Mark?

   _____

THE LORD OF THE RINGS: BOOK FIVE
The Seige of Gondor

1. What honor did Pippin tell Beregond was "a sore trial for a hobbit"?

   _____

   _____

2. What danger did Faramir and his companions face as they made their way to the city's gate, and how were they saved?

   _____

   _____

   _____

   _____

3. If Boromir and Farmir had had their places exchanged, what opportunity did Denethor think Boromir would not have squandered?

   _____

   _____

   _____

4. Gandalf told Pippin that "a traitor may betray himself and do good that he does not intend." Of whom did Gandalf speak and to what treachery did he refer, a treachery that almost caused his heart to fail?

   _____

   _____

   _____

   _____

5. What did Denethor command Faramir to do that was perilous, so much so that Faramir said, "But if I should return, think better of me!"

   _____

   _____

THE LORD OF THE RINGS: BOOK FIVE
The Seige of Gondor, Page 2

6. After Gandalf and the swan-knights of Dol Amroth went out to help the small company returning from Osgiliath, who brought Faramir to the White Tower?

_____

_____

7. The enemy catapulted missles into the first circle of the City that by some secret art burst into flame as they came toppling down. Then what other, smaller shot did they send over the walls that did not burn but which was more horrible?

_____

_____

_____

_____

8. How did Pippin disobey Denethor, following reports of the burning of the first circle of the City?

_____

_____

_____

9. To where did Fen Hollen, located in the wall on the western side of the sixth level of the City, lead and only under what circumstances was it ever unlocked?

_____

_____

_____

_____

10. What choice did Pippin lay before Beregond while the hobbit hurried off to find Gandalf?

_____

_____

11. Named for the mace which Morgoth used in his battle with Fingolf, what was Grond and how was it used?

_____

_____

_____

12. Describe the enemy that first entered the Gate of Gondor and identify who denied this enemy passage into the City.

_____

_____

13. As the cock welcomed the morning, what sound was heard coming from far away, and what did it herald?

_____

_____

_____

_____

THE LORD OF THE RINGS: BOOK FIVE
Project—Fell Beast

Supplies

scissors

paper (heavy cardstock)

glue

Instructions

1. Photocopy onto cardstock or any other sturdy paper.
2. Color the Fell Beast as desired.
3. Cut out along bold lines. Be sure to cut along slits drawn on the neck, as this will allow you to pose the neck. *Adding a pipe cleaner along the inside of the neck area will help the neck to be posed better.*
4. Fold along dotted lines. (In the head this will make a box-like shape).
5. Glue tabs with parallel diagonal lines to the underside of the adjacent areas on the model.
6. Attach wings by gluing tabs onto the contour of the body of the beast. See the photo of the completed model below for guidance.

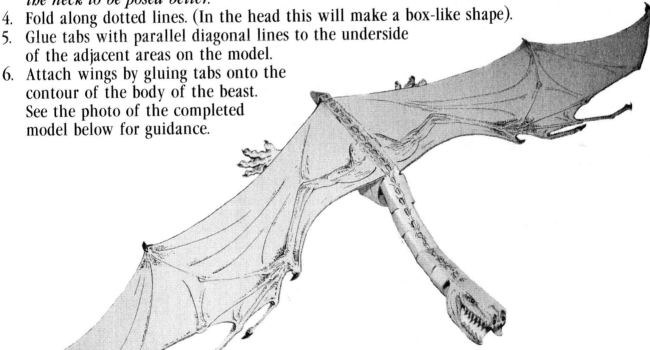

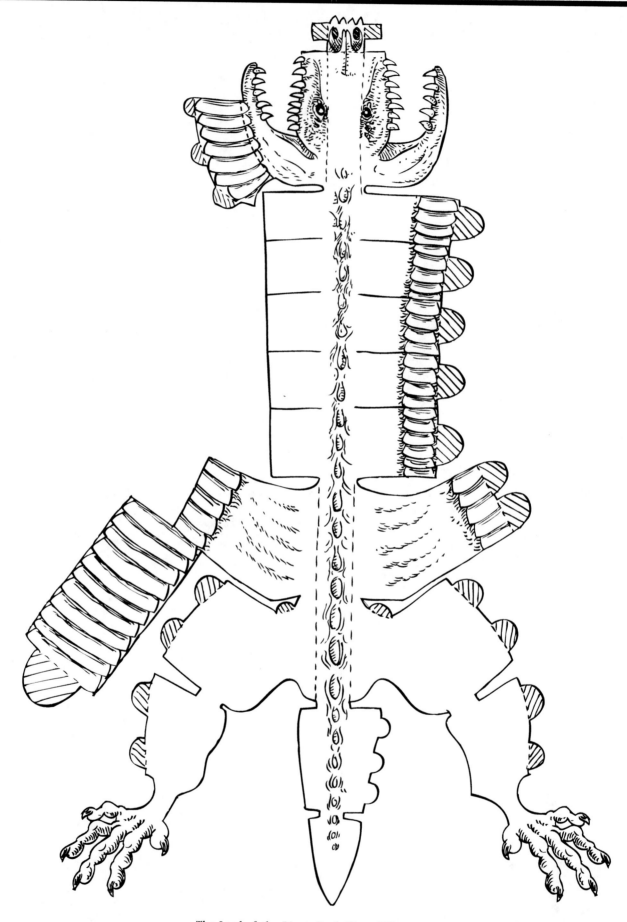

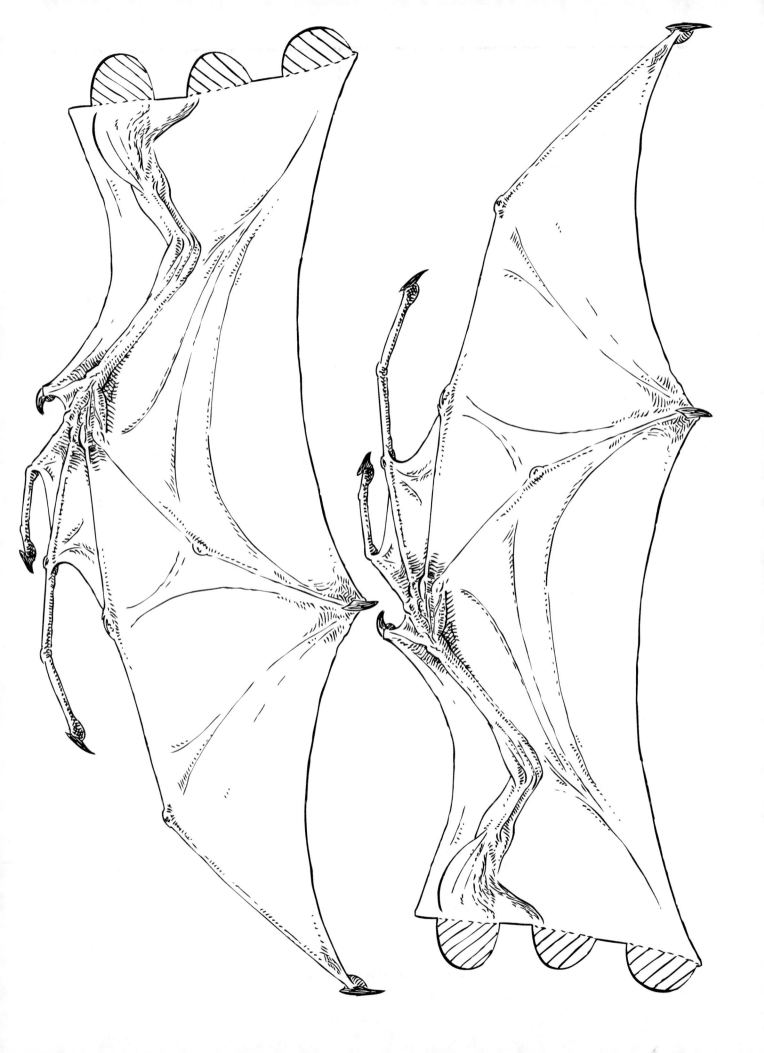

THE LORD OF THE RINGS: BOOK FIVE
The Ride of Rohirrim and *The Battle of the Pelennor Fields*

1. According to Elfhelm the Marshall, who was drumming in the woods?

   _____

   _____

2. Describe Ghân-buri-Ghân.

   _____

   _____

   _____

   _____

3. What arrangement did Théoden make with Ghân-buri-Ghân in return for his aid?

   _____

   _____

   _____

4. What did the scouts report to Théoden that made the king believe that Minas Tirith had not been told of their coming?

   _____

   _____

   _____

5. What rather non-warlike thing did the host of Rohan do while they were killing Orcs?

   _____

   _____

   _____

6. The Witch-King told Dernhelm that "No living man may hinder me!" referring to the prophecy of Glorfindel, "Far off yet is his doom, and not by the hand of man will

he fall." How does Dernhelm get around this prophecy?

_____

_____

_____

7. How did Merry help Dernhelm against the Lord of the Nazgûl?

_____

_____

_____

8. How was Théoden mortally wounded?

_____

_____

_____

9. How did Imrahil save Éowyn?

_____

_____

_____

10. What did Éomer see that made him throw his sword in the air and sing after the sight of the black sails of the Corsairs of Umbar?

_____

_____

_____

THE LORD OF THE RINGS: BOOK FIVE
Project—Riders and Orcs Game

Supplies

Gameboard (two copies of the next page,
 overlapped and taped together so there
 is only one center dot)

Orcs (Eye of Sauron pieces)

Riders of Rohan (horse pieces)

Rules

Two players alternate in placing Orcs and riders on the field/gameboard, with the aim of
surrounding territory. Pieces are never moved, and only removed if they are completely surrounded.

1. Orcs play first. On each turn, a player may place a game piece on any empty *intersection*
    of 2 lines on the board or may pass.
2. *Capturing:* Two points are adjacent if they are next to each other in a vertical or
    horizontal but not diagonal direction. Two pieces of the same color on adjacent points
    are connected and belong to the same string of pieces. An empty point adjacent to a
    string of pieces is a "liberty" of that string. When a piece is played that surrounds the
    opponent's pieces and removes the opponent's liberties, those strings are captured and
    removed from the board.
3. *Illegal Moves:* Suicide—You may not capture your own pieces. A piece may not be played
    if it will have zero liberties and will not capture any of the opponent's pieces.
    Repetition—You may not place a piece on the board if it will make the board look exact-
    ly the same as it did earlier in the game.
4. *Scoring:* If the last move of each player was a pass, the game ends and scoring begins.
    Each player gets one point for every opponent's piece that was captured, and one point
    for every empty point of territory. A group of connected empty points is territory if it is
    surrounded by pieces of only that player's color. The player with the higher score wins.

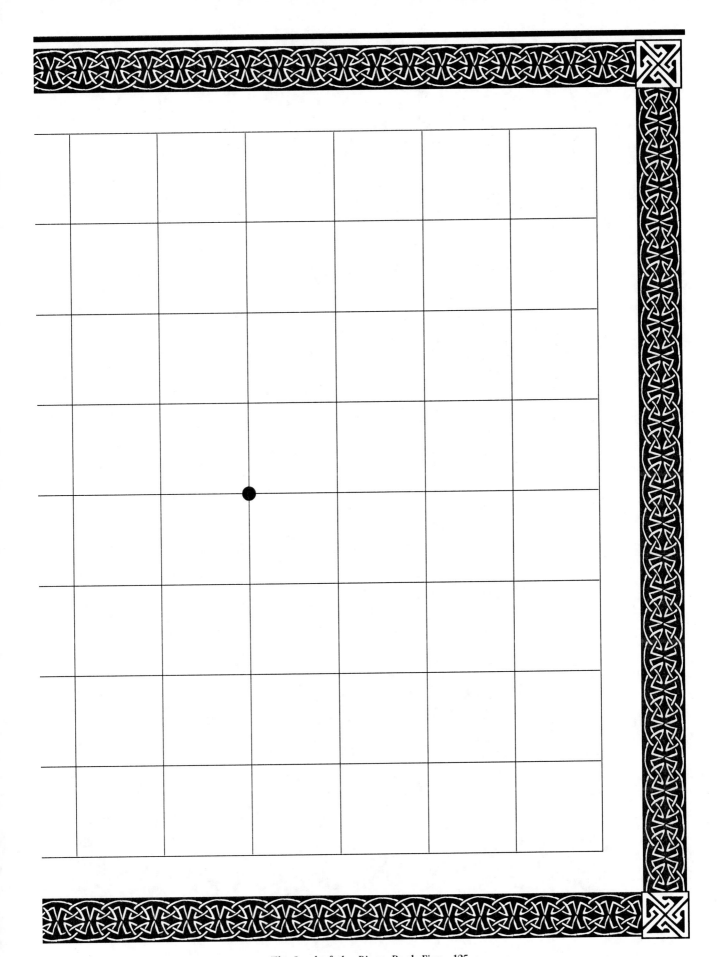

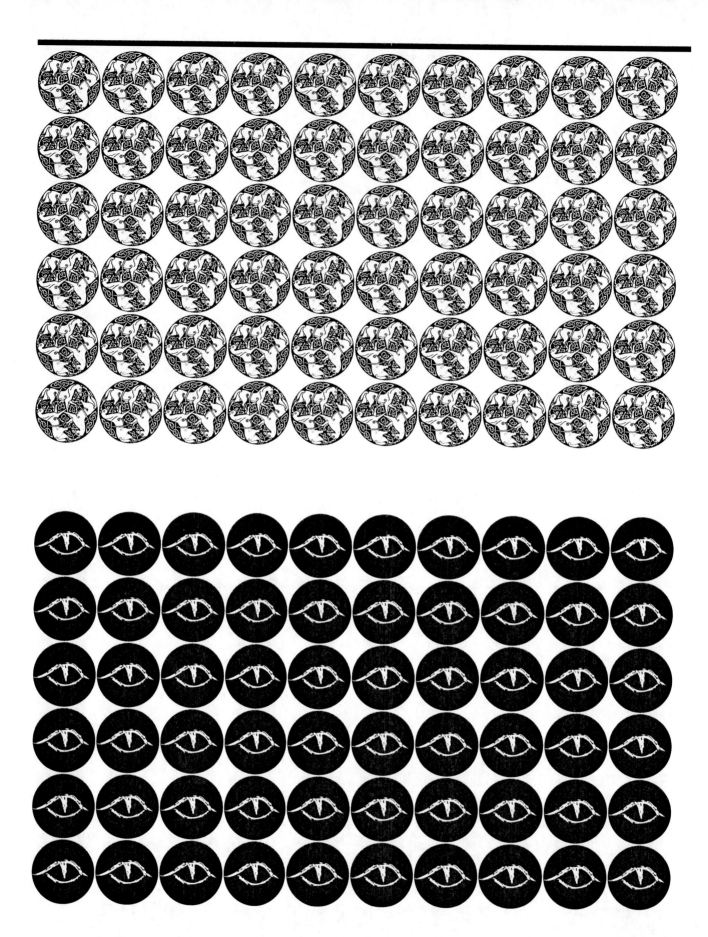

THE LORD OF THE RINGS: BOOK FIVE
Project—Aragorn's Standard

*Following the description in the book,
recreate the standard of Elessar,
Isildur's heir, on the flag below.*

THE LORD OF THE RINGS: BOOK FIVE
The Pyre of Denethor and *The Houses of Healing*

1. Denethor yelled at Gandalf: "Didst thou think that the eyes of the White Tower were blind? Nay, I have seen more than thou knowest, Grey Fool. For thy hope is but ignorance. . . . All the East is moving. And even now the wind of thy hope cheats thee and wafts up Anduin a fleet with black sails. The West has failed." Where did Denethor get his information?

   _____

   _____

   _____

2. How did Denethor die and with whom?

   _____

   _____

   _____

3. Where was Gandalf when the Witch-King was killed?

   _____

   _____

   _____

4. When Pippin found Merry, what did Merry think Pippin was planning to do to him?

   _____

   _____

5. Who was the Captain of the Dúnedain of Arnor, and why did he take this title?

   _____

   _____

   _____

6. Why was Aragorn called by Gandalf into the House of Healing?

_____

_____

7. When Aragorn saw Faramir and Éowyn, he lamented that the eldest of his race was not present to help in the healing. To whom was Aragorn referring?

_____

_____

8. What did Aragorn want Ioreth to run as quick as her tongue to get?

_____

_____

9. What did Éowyn insist that Éomer do to Merry?

_____

_____

10. Why did Merry vow never to smoke again, and what made him change his mind?

_____

_____

_____

_____

11. What name did the people of the City choose for Aragorn?

_____

_____

THE LORD OF THE RINGS: BOOK FIVE
Project—Newspaper Report

Write a front page news article in the Tower Times describing the battle for the family members who had left Minas Tirith before the conflict. You may want to draw a picture of part of the event and paste it over a column or two.

TOWER TIMES

THE LORD OF THE RINGS: BOOK FIVE
The Last Debate and *The Black Gate Opens*

1. If Aragorn was made king at Minas Tirith, what did Gimli and Legolas plan to do for him?

_____

_____

_____

2. What news that Legolas provided did Gimli refuse to share with the hobbits?

_____

_____

3. How did Aragorn defeat the Corsairs of Umbar?

_____

_____

_____

4. What two evil choices did Gandalf set before the sons of Elrond, Éomer, Imrahil and Aragorn?

_____

_____

_____

5. Éomer asked Gandalf during the council in the tents set up near the place Théoden fell why Sauron would attack if Sauron thought that they had the Ring of Power?

_____

_____

6. What was the goal in offering Sauron seven thousand soldiers at his gate as bait?

_____

_____

_____

7. Who of the original Company did Aragorn *not* allow to join the army of the West as they set off to walk open-eyed into Sauron's trap?

_____

_____

8. Why had Gandalf counseled them not to attack Sauron through Minas Morgul?

_____

_____

_____

9. What did Imrahil tell the heralds to proclaim thrice a day instead of "The Lords of Gondor come!"

_____

_____

_____

10. What did Aragorn mercifully command the younger men who were overcome by fear at the sight of the desolate lands lying before Mordor?

_____

_____

_____

THE LORD OF THE RINGS: BOOK FIVE
The Last Debate and *The Black Gate Opens, Page 3*

11. What tokens did the Lieutenant of Barad-dûr offer to Gandalf to show the wizard the failure of his plans?

_____

_____

_____

_____

12. What could Gandalf infer from the Mouth of Sauron about the fate of Frodo and Sam in the negotiating of terms for the release of the "spy from the little rat-land of the Shire"?

_____

_____

_____

_____

13. After thrusting his Westernesse blade into a huge troll and falling under its weight, what did Pippin hear that reminded him of Bilbo?

_____

_____

_____

THE LORD OF THE RINGS: BOOK FIVE
Project—Lego of the Rings

Dig out your old Lego bricks and build the scene of Gandalf negotiating with the Mouth of Sauron at the Black Gate, or some other part of the story. To inspire you, shown here is a Lego Mouth of Sauron and recreation of Frodo at the front door of Bag End.

At the time of printing, these images—and many more—could be found at http://www.brickshelf.com/cgi-bin/gallery.cgi?f=9222

THE LORD OF THE RINGS: BOOK FIVE
Project—Timeline

How well have you been paying attention? Test your comprehension by filling in this timeline.

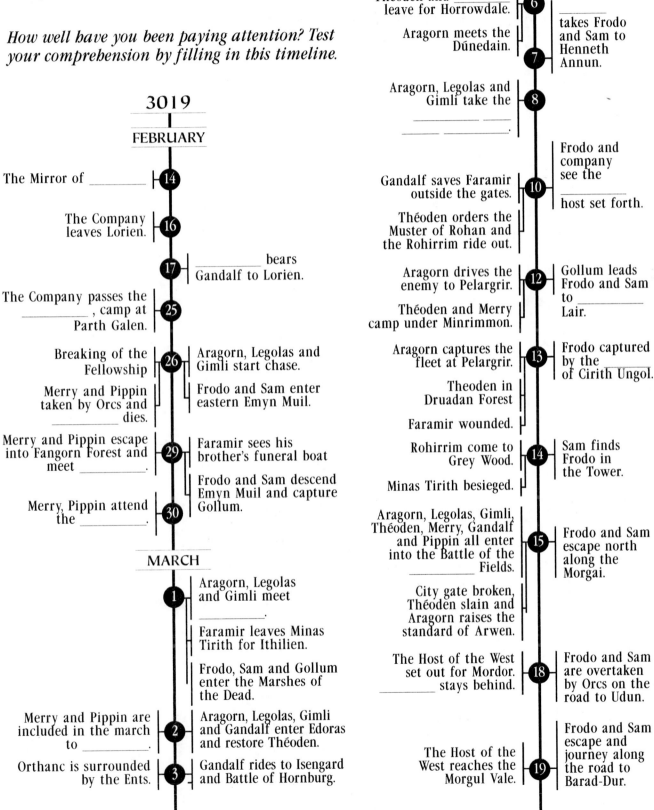

3019

FEBRUARY

14 — The Mirror of _____

16 — The Company leaves Lorien.

17 — _____ bears Gandalf to Lorien.

25 — The Company passes the _____, camp at Parth Galen.

26 — Breaking of the Fellowship
Merry and Pippin taken by Orcs and _____ dies.
Aragorn, Legolas and Gimli start chase.
Frodo and Sam enter eastern Emyn Muil.

29 — Merry and Pippin escape into Fangorn Forest and meet _____.
Faramir sees his brother's funeral boat
Frodo and Sam descend Emyn Muil and capture Gollum.

30 — Merry, Pippin attend the _____.

MARCH

1 — Aragorn, Legolas and Gimli meet _____.
Faramir leaves Minas Tirith for Ithilien.
Frodo, Sam and Gollum enter the Marshes of the Dead.

2 — Merry and Pippin are included in the march to _____.
Aragorn, Legolas, Gimli and Gandalf enter Edoras and restore Théoden.

3 — Orthanc is surrounded by the Ents.
Gandalf rides to Isengard and Battle of Hornburg.

5 — Gandalf and Pippin leave for _____.

MARCH

6 — Théoden and _____ leave for Horrowdale.

7 — Aragorn meets the Dúnedain.
_____ takes Frodo and Sam to Henneth Annun.

8 — Aragorn, Legolas and Gimli take the _____ _____.

10 — Gandalf saves Faramir outside the gates.
Théoden orders the Muster of Rohan and the Rohirrim ride out.
Frodo and company see the _____ host set forth.

12 — Aragorn drives the enemy to Pelargrir.
Théoden and Merry camp under Minrimmon.
Gollum leads Frodo and Sam to _____ Lair.

13 — Aragorn captures the fleet at Pelargrir.
Theoden in Druadan Forest
Faramir wounded.
Frodo captured by the _____ of Cirith Ungol.

14 — Rohirrim come to Grey Wood.
Minas Tirith besieged.
Sam finds Frodo in the Tower.

15 — Aragorn, Legolas, Gimli, Théoden, Merry, Gandalf and Pippin all enter into the Battle of the _____ Fields.
City gate broken, Théoden slain and Aragorn raises the standard of Arwen.
Frodo and Sam escape north along the Morgai.

18 — The Host of the West set out for Mordor. _____ stays behind.
Frodo and Sam are overtaken by Orcs on the road to Udun.

19 — The Host of the West reaches the Morgul Vale.
Frodo and Sam escape and journey along the road to Barad-Dur.

THE LORD OF THE RINGS: BOOK SIX
The Tower of Cirith Ungol

1. At the beginning of Book Six, where do we find Sam?

   _____

   _____

2. What effect did wearing the Ring have on Sam's senses?

   _____

   _____

   _____

3. The Tower of Cirith Ungol was built by the Men of Gondor after Sauron was defeated in the War of the Last Alliance at the end of the Second Age. What was its original purpose, and why had Sauron found it useful?

   _____

   _____

   _____

   _____

THE LORD OF THE RINGS: BOOK SIX
The Tower of Cirith Ungol, Page 2

4. What helped Sam conquer his fantasies of Samwise the Strong, Hero of the Age?

_____

_____

_____

5. How was Sam able to get by the Two Watchers?

_____

_____

_____

6. What did Sam do when he got to a dead end without finding Frodo?

_____

_____

_____

7. What did Frodo call Sam as Sam returned the Ring?

_____

_____

8. What did Frodo insist that they do before they left the top of the tower where he had been kept?

_____

_____

THE LORD OF THE RINGS: BOOK SIX
The Land of the Shadow

1. For what would Sam be willing to shake even Shagrat's hand?

   _____

   _____

   _____

   _____

2. What would Sam ask of Galadriel, if he could, that would be better than any jewels?

   _____

   _____

   _____

   _____

   _____

3. While Frodo slept, what did Sam see far above Ephel Dúath in the West, the beauty of which smote his heart?

   _____

   _____

   _____

   _____

   _____

4. What did Sam and Frodo learn from eavesdropping on the conversation of a small tracker Orc and a large soldier Orc?

_____

_____

_____

_____

5. What did Sam catch sight of while off getting water?

_____

_____

6. What happened to Frodo and Sam when a company of Orcs came upon them?

_____

_____

_____

7. How did the two hobbits escape the Orcs?

_____

_____

_____

THE LORD OF THE RINGS: BOOK SIX
Mount Doom

1. When the chapter begins, how long did Sam think it would take for them to reach Orodruin, that is, Mount Doom?

   _____

   _____

2. What happened to Sam as he realized that they wouldn't have enough provisions to make it back home after they reached the volcano?

   _____

   _____

   _____

   _____

3. What did they discard along with their Orc gear, the parting from which brought Sam to tears?

   _____

   _____

4. How did they make any progress towards the Cracks of Doom once Frodo was reduced to crawling towards the foot of the mountain?

   _____

   _____

5. Sam and Frodo stumbled onto a road that led up to Sammath Naur—the Chambers of Fire. Where did the other end of the road lead?

   _____

   _____

6. Who ambushed Sam and Frodo as they followed the last part of the road to the right onto the eastern side of Orodruin?

_____

_____

7. What punishment did Frodo prophecy against his attacker before continuing up the path alone?

_____

_____

_____

8. What violent act was Sam restrained from doing by something deep in his heart?

_____

_____

9. What happened as soon as Frodo claimed the Ring for himself?

_____

_____

_____

_____

10. How did Frodo lose the Ring?

_____

_____

_____

THE LORD OF THE RINGS: BOOK SIX
The One Ring Game

For 3 to 5 players, ages 10 and up

CARDS

Cut out the cards from this guide or photocopy the cards onto cardstock with the knotwork backing up each card, then cut out. You should end up with:

14 Eye of Sauron Cards
14 White Tree Cards
3 Rings of Power Cards

PAWNS

Photocopy the pawns onto cardstock. Cut along the solid lines, fold the dashed lines and glue or tape the triangular tabs inside the square panels to create cubes. You should end up with:

4 Dwarves
4 Elves
4 Hobbits
3 Gollums
1 Gandalf
1 The One Ring

GAMEBOARD

The gameboard is a long narrow panel. Each of the following pages overlap the preceeding page slightly. The Mount Doom drawing is based on an actual illustration of the volcano made by J.R.R. Tolkien.

SETUP

Place the One Ring on the blank Mount Doom space.

Each player chooses a set of pawns. Each player puts one of his pawns in front of himself to mark which character he is.

Shuffle the cards and deal five to each player.

The youngest player goes first. Play proceeds clockwise from there.

GAMEPLAY

On each turn, a player does two things, in this order:

- Plays one card from his hand and moves the One Ring.
- Places one of his pawns on the board, *except:* Gollum does not place a pawn on his first turn and Gandalf never places a pawn.

Playing a Card and Moving the One Ring:

When a card is played, the One Ring is moved. Eye of Sauron cards move the One Ring toward the Eye of Sauron gate (space 17); White Tree cards move the One Ring toward the White Tree gate (space 17).

For example, if an Eye of Sauron 4 is played first, the One Ring moves from Mount Doom to the Eye of Sauron 4 space on the board. If an Eye of Sauron 6 is played next, the One Ring moves from the Eye of Sauron 4 space to the Eye of Sauron 10 space. If a

THE LORD OF THE RINGS: BOOK SIX
The One Ring Game

White Tree 5 is played next, the One Ring moves from the Eye of Sauron 10 space to the Eye of Sauron 5 space. When the ring crosses Mount Doom, Mount Doom is counted as a space. It is possible for the ring to stop on Mount Doom during the game.

Rings of Power Cards:
When a Rings of Power card is played, the player chooses which direction to move the One Ring, and he may move it either 4 or 5 spaces in that direction.

Placing a pawn:
If the player taking his turn controls the dwarves, elves or hobbits, he places a pawn on an empty space that is not already surrounded by pawns. (A space is surrounded if pawns have already been placed on both sides of it.)

Gollum places a pawn on an empty space that is not already surrounded by pawns. *Remember:* Gollum does not place a pawn on his first turn.

Gandalf never places a pawn. Gandalf only scores if the One Ring is on or near Mount Doom at the end of a round.

Only one pawn is permitted per space. Two pawns can never occupy the same space. However, it is permitted for a pawn to share a space with the One Ring.

Designed by Erik Arneson
Inspired by Dragon Parade (Reiner Knizia, Z-Man Games, 2006)

ROUND ENDS

There are two ways for a round to end.

Normally, the round ends after each player has played three cards.

Occasionally, the round will end immediately if the One Ring leaves either end of the game board. This should be rare, but it can happen.

Note: If the round ends in this manner, normal scoring does not take place. Instead, Gollum earns +5 points.

SCORING

Gollum earns +4 for each pawn within three spaces of the ring. However, he scores nothing if the One Ring ends the game on Mount Doom.

The Dwarves, Elves and Hobbits earn +3 for each pawn on the side of the board opposite the One Ring. However, they score nothing if the One Ring ends the game on Mount Doom.

Gandalf earns +10 if the One Ring ends on Mount Doom, and +5 if the One Ring is within four spaces of Mount Doom, on either side.

MULTIPLE ROUNDS

A full game includes as many rounds as there are players. It's best, although not required, for the players to be different characters each game.

Scores are added cumulatively to determine the winner.

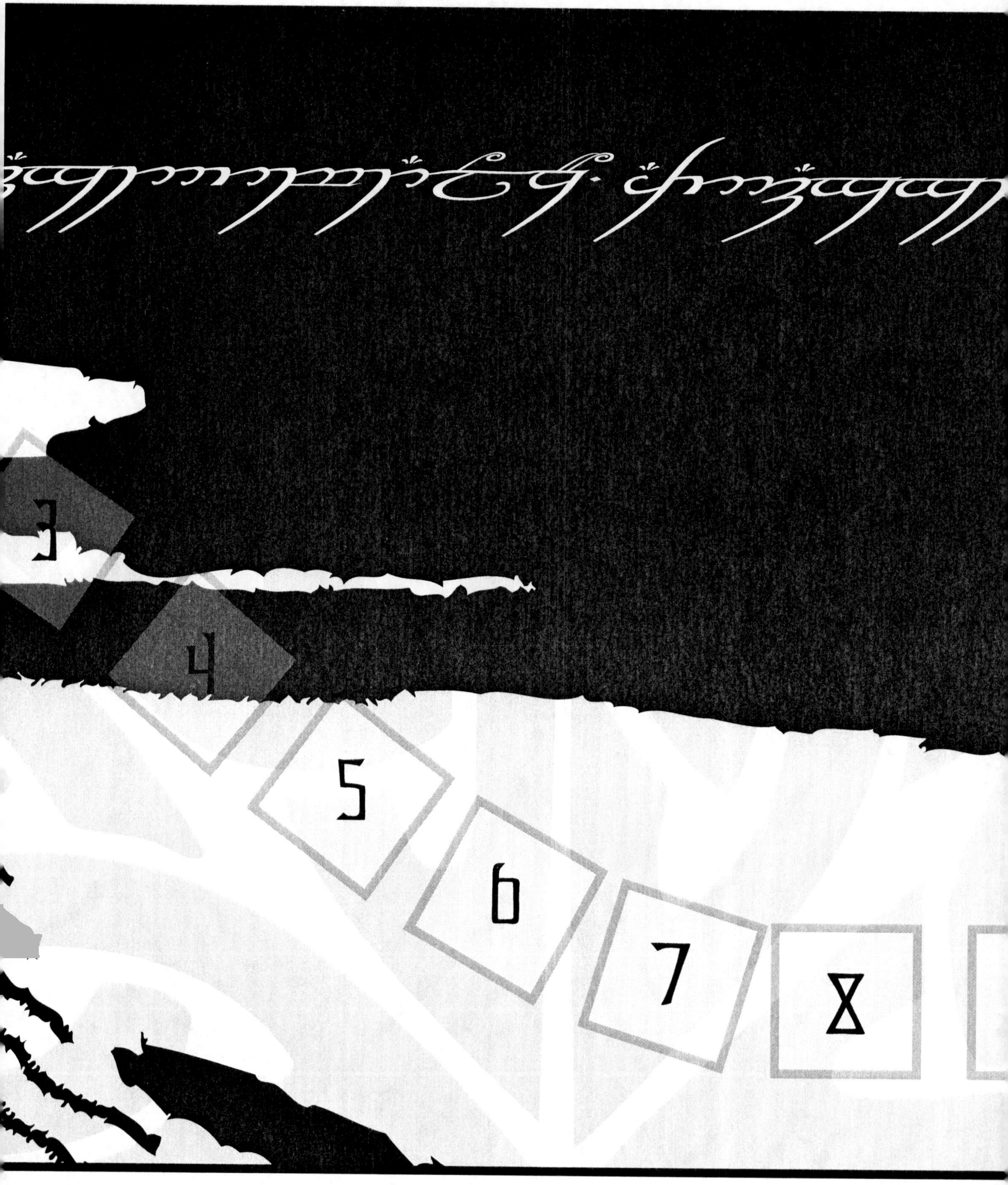

3
4
5
6
7
8

9 10 11 12 13 1

14 15 16 17

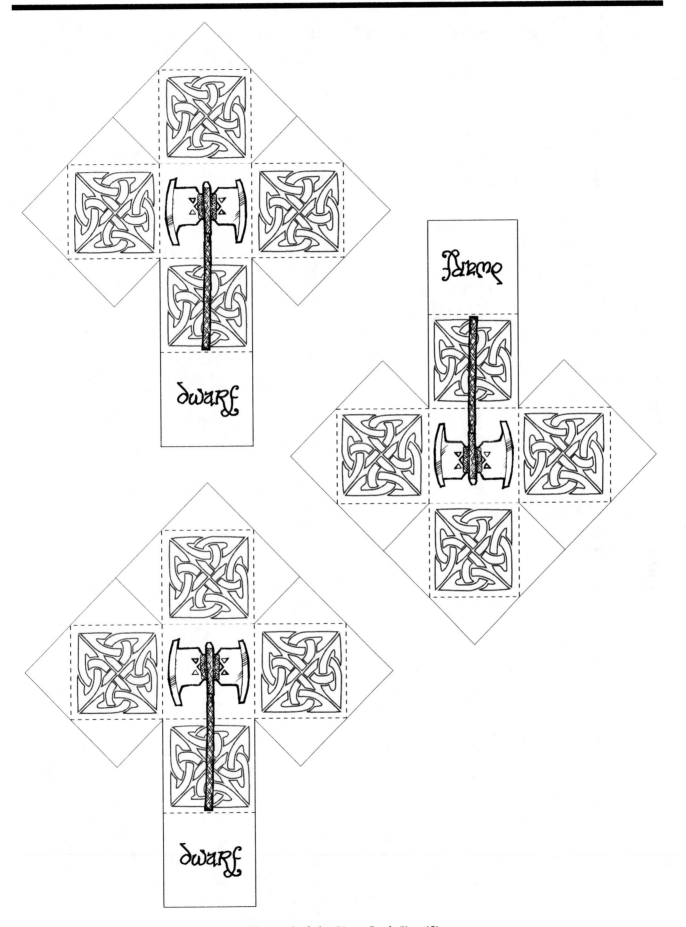

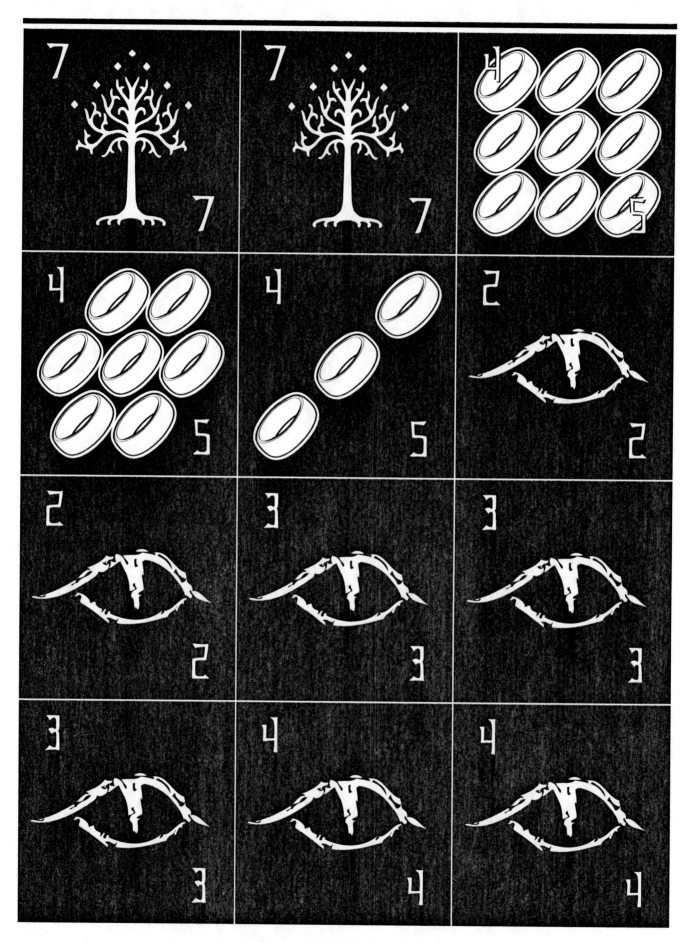

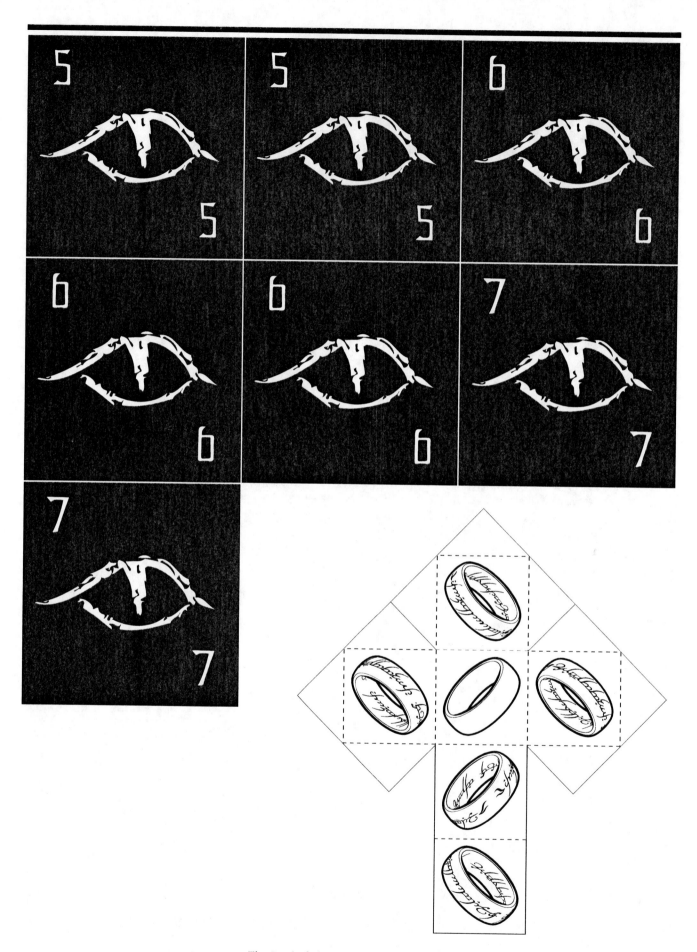

The Lord of the Rings: Book Six · 156

dwarf

The Lord of the Rings: Book Six · 157

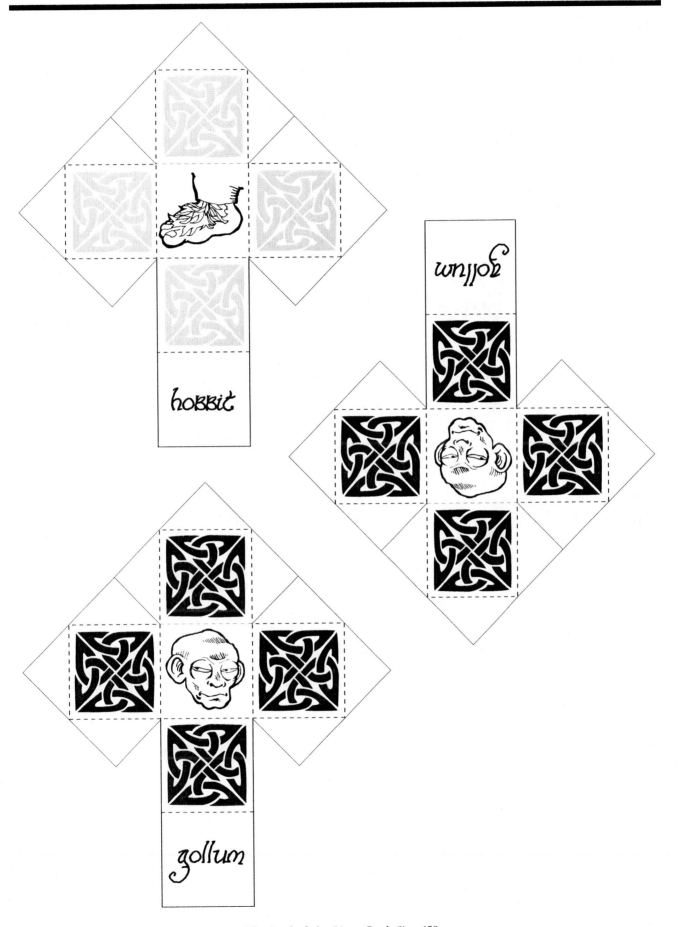

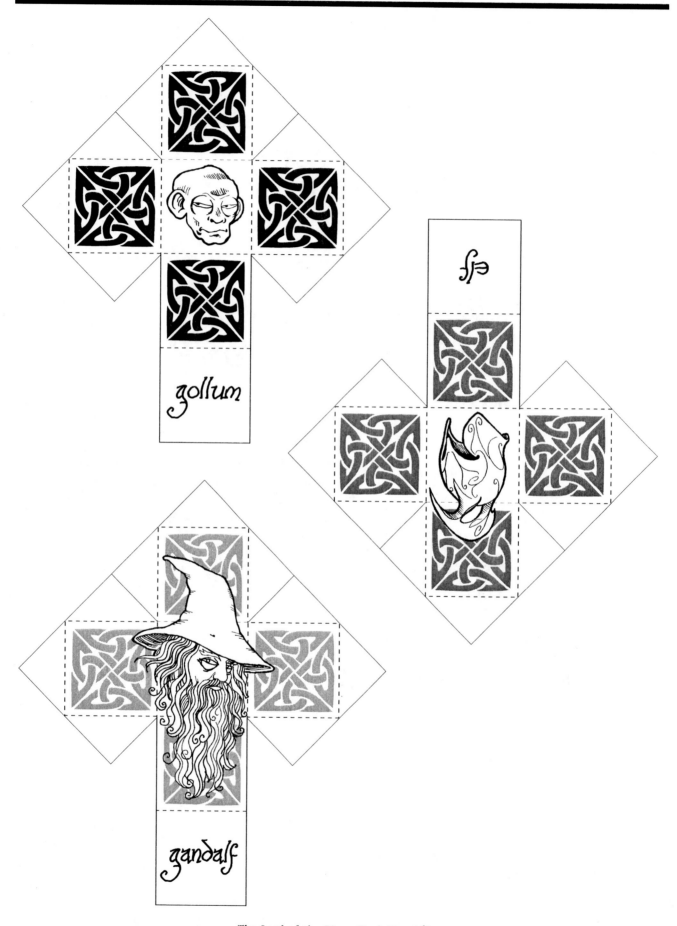

gollum

gandalf

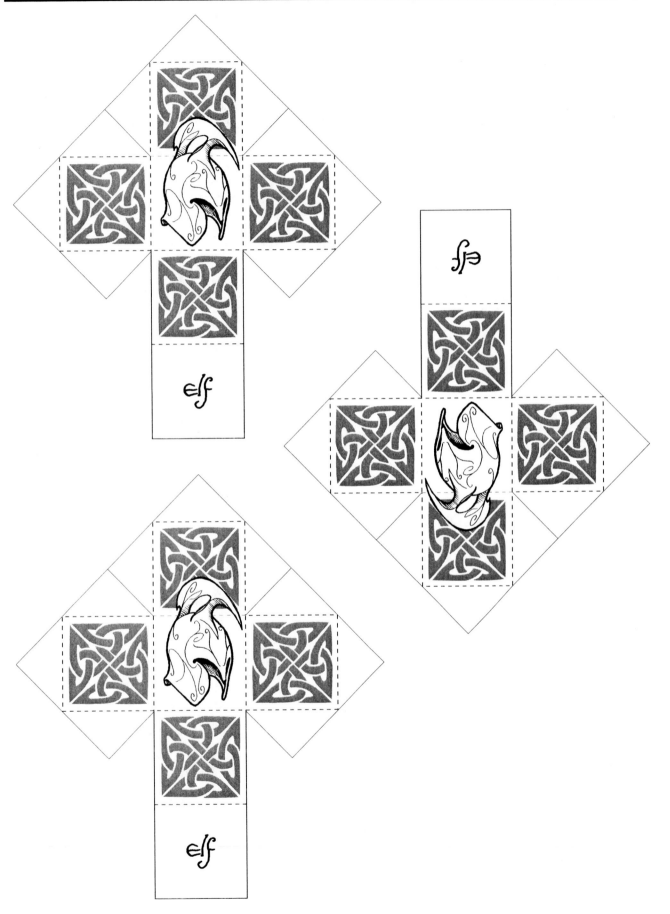

THE LORD OF THE RINGS: BOOK SIX
The Field of Cormallen

1. What did Gandalf see that made him say, "The realm of Sauron is ended"?

   _____

   _____

   _____

   _____

2. Following this eucatastrophe (a word Tolkien coined to refer to "the sudden happy turn in a story which pierces you with a joy that brings tears"), while Sam and Frodo sat on an island amid the torment of Orodruin, what did Gandalf ask of Gwaihir?

   _____

   _____

   _____

3. After waking to the smell of Ithilien, what was Sam's reaction when Gandalf laughs?

   _____

   _____

4. When the hobbits were brought before the king, what happened that made Sam exclaim, "O great glory and spleandour! And all my wishes have come true," and then weep?

   _____

   _____

   _____

5. Later, at the feast, who was Sam surprised to see serving the King's table?

   _____

   _____

6. What creature was Sam disappointed that he missed seeing, while he was off with Frodo?

   _____

   _____

THE LORD OF THE RINGS: BOOK SIX
The Steward and the King

1. What was it that Éowyn desired that the Warden of the Houses of Healing denied?

   _____

   _____

2. How did Faramir think Éowyn could ease the Steward's care?

   _____

   _____

   _____

   _____

3. How did Merry serve Faramir in regards to the Lady of Rohan?

   _____

   _____

   _____

4. What happened the day that Faramir wrapped Éowyn in the starry mantle of Finduilas?

   _____

   _____

   _____

   _____

5. What two possibilities did Faramir suggest as reasons for Éowyn not joining Éomer in Cormallen?

   _____

   _____

   _____

   _____

THE LORD OF THE RINGS: BOOK SIX
The Steward and the King

6. Éowyn queried Faramir, "Then must I leave my own people, man of Gondor? . . . And would you have your proud folk say of you: 'There goes a lord who tamed a wild shield-maiden of the North! Was there no woman of the race of Numenor to choose?'" What did Faramir answer, and what did he do that led the Warden to release her from the Houses of Healing?

_____

_____

_____

_____

_____

_____

_____

_____

_____

7. Who prattled on during the ceremony welcoming the return of the King?

_____

_____

8. Describe the crown of Eärnur and indicate who it was that crowned Aragorn.

_____

_____

_____

_____

9. What punishment did King Elessar mete out on Beregond for leaving his post and for killing the porter and Denethor's servants on hallowed ground?

_____

_____

_____

_____

10. What sign did Gandalf show Aragorn on the Mount Mindolluin that gave him hope for the future line of Kings?

_____

_____

_____

11. What happened of which Frodo said, "This is the ending"?

_____

_____

THE LORD OF THE RINGS: BOOK SIX
Project—A Love Story

In 1963, a fan sent a letter to Tolkien that was critical of the rapid and "unrealistic" love story between Éowyn and Faramir in light of Éowyn's love for Aragorn. Tolkien's defense was that her feelings for Aragorn and Faramir were very different: "It is possible to love more than one person (of the other sex) at the same time, but in a different mode and intensity. I do not think that Éowyn's feelings for Aragorn really changed much; and when he was revealed as so lofty a figure, in descent and office, she was able to go on loving and admiring him." He also wrote that: "In my experience feelings and decisions ripen very quickly (as measured by mere 'clock-time,' which is actually not justly applicable) in periods of great stress, and especially under the expectation of imminent death." *Write a short essay defending or criticizing the author's handling of Éowyn and Faramir's courtship.*

THE LORD OF THE RINGS: BOOK SIX
Many Partings and *Homeward Bound*

1. What gift did the Queen give to Frodo?

_____

_____

_____

2. Why did Éomer ask Gimli to get his axe, and why did the dwarf excuse him?

_____

_____

_____

_____

3. What did King Elessar give to the Woses to be theirs forever?

_____

_____

_____

4. What did Éomer give to Éowyn at the funeral feast of Théoden, and what did Éowyn ask for from Aragorn?

_____

_____

_____

5. What did Éowyn insist on giving to Merry?

_____

_____

_____

THE LORD OF THE RINGS: BOOK SIX
Many Partings and *Homeward Bound, Page 2*

6. How did Gimli claim a victory over Legolas in the Glittering Caves?

_____

_____

_____

7. Where did the Fellowship of the Ring come to its final ending?

_____

_____

_____

8. What was Treebeard's final request of Merry and Pippin?

_____

_____

_____

9. What did Saruman say that made Merry take back his leather pipeweed pouch?

_____

_____

_____

10. What part of the hobbit's account of their adventures truly held the attention of Bilbo?

_____

_____

_____

_____

THE LORD OF THE RINGS: BOOK SIX
Many Partings and *Homeward Bound, Page 3*

11. What gifts did Bilbo give to the hobbits?

_____

_____

_____

_____

12. Since the hobbits had first been through Bree, there had been some bad trouble, with some people even getting killed! What did Butterbur say was the death count?

_____

_____

_____

13. As Butterbur bemoaned more comings and goings on the Greenway and outsiders coming to his inn, what news made him gasp and stare in wonder?

_____

_____

_____

14. What reunion in Bree cheered Sam the most?

_____

_____

15. Instead of returning to the Shire with the hobbits, what moss-gatherer did Gandalf go to visit?

_____

_____

THE LORD OF THE RINGS: BOOK SIX
Project—A Letter from Rivendell

In the calligraphic style of hobbits (shown below), write a letter from the son of Bungo Baggins to his old friend the Dúnadan, congratulating him on his recent nuptials and new job.

ä B c d e f g h i j k l m n o p q R S t u v w x y z

THE LORD OF THE RINGS: BOOK SIX
The Scouring of the Shire

1. Who was the "big man" that Merry scared off at the gate at Brandywine bridge?

   _____

   _____

2. Frodo was "arrested" near Frogmorton for Gate-breaking, Tearing up of Rules, Assaulting Gate-keepers, Trespassing, Sleeping in Shire-buildings without Leave and Bribing Guards with Food. What infractions did Sam wish to add to that list?

   _____

   _____

   _____

3. After Pippin scared off the thugs at *The Green Dragon,* who did Frodo declare that they should rescue, much to the surprise of Pippin?

   _____

   _____

4. As Merry was sounding his horn and calling hobbits to action, what did Sam stop to do?

   _____

   _____

5. Pimple was bad but Sharkey was worse. What did Farmer Cotton share about Sandyman's mill as an example of this?

   _____

   _____

   _____

   _____

   _____

6. Describe the Battle of Bywater.

_____

_____

_____

_____

7. When Frodo, Sam, Merry and Pippin marched up to Bag End and saw the awful devastation, what sight was the "last straw" that brought Sam to tears?

_____

_____

8. What did Frodo do to the *sharkû* that robbed him of the sweetness of his revenge?

_____

_____

9. What was the fate of Lotho and the Pimple's attacker?

_____

_____

_____

10. What happened to the body of Saruman in the end?

_____

_____

_____

THE LORD OF THE RINGS
Project—Restoring the Shire

"This is worse than Mordor!" said Sam. "Much worse in a way. It comes home to you, as they say; because it's home, and you remember it before it was all ruined."

When Frodo, Sam, Merry and Pippin arrived at Bywater they were shocked to see:

Many of the houses that they had known were missing. Some seemed to have been burned down. The pleasant row of old hobbit-holes in the bank on the north side of the Pool were deserted, and their little gardens that used to run down right to the water's edge were rank with weeds. Worse, there was a whole line of ugly new houses all along the Pool side, where the Hobbiton Road ran close to the bank. An avenue of trees had stood there. They were all gone. And looking with dismay up the road towards Bag End they saw a tall chimney of brick in the distance. It was pouring out black smoke into the evening air.

And at Bag End they saw that the old mill had been torn down and a larger one built in its place, Bagshot row had been dug up into a quarry, fields were bare of grass, huts had been erected in front of Bag End, and (for Sam the worst sight of all) the Party Tree had been cut down and lay rotting in the field. As Sam observed, there was quite a mess to clean up which would require much time and work—the fruit of which would likely only be seen by his great grandchildren.

Although not included in Jackson's film adaptaion of the book, the Scouring and rebuilding of the Shire is central to Tolkien's vision. In *Ents, Elves and Eriador: The Environmental Vision of J.R.R. Tolkien*, Matthew Dickerson and Jonathan Evans write: "The narrative of the hobbits' repair and restoration of the Shire should be seen not as an afterthought but as central to the whole tale. [The chapter is a] portrayal of the author's environmental vision." Although not what would be called an environmentalist by today's popular definition, Tolkien consciously wrote in a way that would "take the part of the trees against all their enemies" (*Letters*, 419).

Looking at the world around us we can find places that are "worse than Mordor." Discuss little ways that you could begin to restore your corner of "the Shire." You might begin by thinking about what it would look like to eat like a hobbit.

THE LORD OF THE RINGS: BOOK SIX
The Grey Havens

1. What was one of the first things done to restore Hobbiton?

   _____

   _____

2. What became of Galadriel's gift to Sam?

   _____

   _____

   _____

   _____

   _____

3. What did Sam do in the Spring of 1420 before moving in to live at Bag End?

   _____

   _____

   _____

4. What name did Frodo suggest for Sam's first-born?

   _____

   _____

5. Frodo and Sam traveled east the same way they had when they first met Gildor. On September 22nd, whom did they meet on that same road?

   _____

   _____

   _____

THE LORD OF THE RINGS: BOOK SIX
The Grey Havens, Page 2

6. Who met the travelers at the gates of the Grey Havens?

_____

_____

7. What were Gandalf's final words to the hobbits?

_____

_____

_____

_____

THE LORD OF THE RINGS: BOOK SIX
The Grey Havens, Project—The Book vs. the Movie

After watching Peter Jackson's movie The Return of the King, *answer the following questions concerning differences between the books and the movie.*

1. In the movie the Rohirrim ride all night to reach Minas Tirith, skipping their meeting with whom?

   _____

   _____

   _____

2. In the Extended DVD cut Éowyn is shown to be healed by Aragorn, but in the book who else does Aragorn heal as well?

   _____

   _____

3. During Aragorn's coronation the courtyard is covered by the blossoms, and the White Tree is seen in the background in full bloom. How is the restoration of the White Tree different in the book?

   _____

   _____

   _____

   _____

4. In the movie, Gollum tricks Frodo into not trusting Sam and sends him away right before entering Shelob's Lair. How is this a significant change from the book?

   _____

   _____

   _____

   _____

5. In the movie the city of Minas Tirith is brimming with women and children during the Siege of Gondor, but what happened to the women and children in the book?

_____

_____

_____

6. The Outer Walls of Minas Tirith were virtually impregnable, but in the movie what becomes of them?

_____

_____

_____

7. In the movie at the Black Gate the Mouth of Sauron is decapitated by Aragorn with the reforged Andúril. How is this different from the book?

_____

_____

_____

8. In the book, the beacons of Gondor are lit as a part of Denethor's careful mustering of Minas Tirith's defences. Who lights the beacons in the movie?

_____

_____

_____

_____

_____

9. In the book, the Rangers of the North, Legolas, Gimli, and Aragorn ride through the mountain path to summon the Dead, then ride through the Morthond valley to the stone of Erech, where the Dead agree to serve. In the movie who is missing from this scene?

_____

_____

_____

10. In the book, Gollum falls accidentally into the Crack of Doom while dancing in triumph, but what happens to Gollum in the movie?

_____

_____

_____

_____

11. In the movie, Gandalf confronts Saruman at Isengard, where the bent wizard meets a grizzly death. In perhaps the most significant change made by Peter Jackson, what events at the end of the book are missing from the movie pertaining to Saruman?

_____

_____

_____

_____

THE LORD OF THE RINGS: APPENDIX A
Annals of the Kings and Rulers

1. Who made the *Silmarilli* and filled them with the radiance of Telperion and Laurelin?

    _____

    _____

2. What was the "Ban of the Valar," and how was it part of the downfall of Númenor?

    _____

    _____

    _____

    _____

3. What lie did Sauron speak to Ar-Pharazôn the Golden, and what was the disasterous result?

    _____

    _____

    _____

    _____

4. According to some, how did the grave of the last prince of Cardolan factor into Frodo's journey in *The Fellowship of the Ring?*

    _____

    _____

5. Where were the ring of Barahir, the shards of Narsil, the star of Elendil and the sceptre of Annúminas kept after the North-kingdom ended?

    _____

    _____

6. Why did Strider never enter the Shire after becoming king?

_____

_____

7. What hobbit became a maid of honor to Arwen?

_____

_____

8. When King Telemnar died, so did the White Trees of Minas Anor, so how did it come that a white tree grew in the citadel of Minas Tirith (originally named Minas Anor)?

_____

_____

_____

9. Denethor was not the first to reject a direct descendant of Isildur as king. Who rejected Arvedui's claim and on what grounds?

_____

_____

_____

_____

10. What happened when Belecthor II, the twenty-first Steward of Gondor, died?

_____

_____

_____

11. During the reign of Ecthelion II, son of Turgon, Aragorn served to strengthen Gondor against Mordor, even leading an attack against the Corsairs and overthrowing the Captain of the Haven. The people of Gondor called him the Eagle of the Star, but what name did Ecthelion know him as?

_____

_____

12. How did Denethor gain knowledge of things beyond his realm, in a way that not even the kings Eärnil and Eärnur dared?

_____

_____

13. Who are Estel and Undómiel, and how did they meet?

_____

_____

_____

14. Under what condition was Elrond willing to see his daughter marry a man?

_____

_____

_____

15. Where did Lady Evenstar die?

_____

_____

16. What did Eorl rename Mansbane, and who was Mansbane's famous descendant?

_____

_____

17. In the end, men realized that Saruman became warden of Isengard not out of friendship but in hopes of what?

_____

_____

_____

18. How did King Éomer often fulfill the Oath of Eorl?

_____

_____

_____

19. During the reign of Durin VI, what unintentional side effect came from digging beneath Barazinbar for mithril?

_____

_____

_____

20. What was the fate of Thrór in Moria?

_____

_____

_____

21. How did Thorin gain the epithet "Oakenshield" at the Battle of Azanulbizar?

_____

_____

_____

22. Who was the Lord of the Glittering Caves, and what unusual grace was extended to him following the death of King Elessar?

_____

_____

_____

_____

THE LORD OF THE RINGS: APPENDIX B
The Tale of Years

1. Who were the *Istari?* Where did they come from, and what did they look like?

_____

_____

_____

_____

_____

2. Who gave Gandalf the Ring of Fire and for what purpose?

_____

_____

_____

3. Following the fall of the Dark Tower, who led the host of Lórien Anduin to take Dol Guldur and clean the forest?

_____

_____

_____

4. What happened to Sam and Pippin in 1427?

_____

_____

_____

_____

THE LORD OF THE RINGS: APPENDIX B
The Tale of Years, Page 2

5. Who sent gifts to Merry when he was made Master of Buckland?

_____

_____

_____

6. What happened to Pippin in the year that Sam was reelected Mayor of the Shire?

_____

_____

_____

7. What did Sam do after Rose died?

_____

_____

_____

_____

8. Where did Merry and Pippin spend their final days?

_____

_____

_____

THE LORD OF THE RINGS
Vocabulary

By consulting a dictionary, define the following words found in The Lord of the Rings. *It would be very helpful to the reader to complete each Book's vocabulary list before reading that section of the story.*

BOOK ONE

imbibe

_____

provender

_____

coppice

_____

tussocky

_____

bollard

_____

hoary

_____

barrow

_____

wight

_____

russet

_____

standing stone

_____

damask

_____

sallow

_____

quagmire

_____

wraith

_____

cairn

_____

BOOK TWO

panoply

_____

habergeon

_____

chalcedony

_____

carcanet

_____

errantry

_____

baldric

_____

tryst

_____

sylvan

_____

faggot

_____

bole

_____

ewer

_____

hythe

_____

fen

_____

phial

_____

wold

_____

eyot

_____

sloe

_____

BOOK THREE

escarpment

_____

craven

_____

splayed

_____

dingle

_____

eyrie

_____

cleave

_____

sedge

_____

coomb

_____

parapet

_____

flotsam

_____

jetsam

_____

flounder

_____

dotard

_____

remonstrance

_____

bracken

_____

BOOK FOUR

spate

_____

bight

_____

pinion

_____

gangrel

_____

elixir

_____

foundered

_____

canker

_____

gorse

_____

charnel

_____

fey

_____

doughty

_____

orb

_____

lubber

_____

BOOK FIVE

oast

_____

byre

_____

thain

_____

wroth

_____

pyre

_____

baluster

_____

doggrel

_____

trammel

_____

ghyll

_____

feint

_____

scree

_____

scouring

_____

grist

_____

weskit

_____

dawdling

_____

shale

_____

firth

_____

BOOK SIX

turves

_____

presage

_____

puissant

_____

cudgel

_____

THE LORD OF THE RINGS
Project—Athrabeth Finrod Ah Andreth

Athrabeth Finrod ah Andreth or *The Debate of Finrod and Andreth* is a story in *Morgoth's Ring* (pp. 303–366), the tenth volume of *The History of Middle-earth*, a story that was originally supposed to be part of *The Silmarillion*. In it, Finrod Felagund, an Elven King, and Andreth, a mortal woman, discuss, among other things, the differences between Elves and Men. *Read the following selection from* The Debate of Finrod and Andreth *and discuss the questions at the end of the excerpt.*

"Have ye then no hope" said Finrod.

"What is hope" she said. "An expectation of good, which though uncertain has some foundation in what is known? Then we have none."

"That is one thing that Men call 'hope'," said Finrod. "*Amdir* we call it, 'looking up'. But there is another which is founded deeper. *Estel* we call it, that is 'trust'. It is not defeated by the ways of the world, for it does not come from experience, but from our nature and first being. If we are indeed the *Eruhin*, the Children of the One,[1] then He will not suffer Himself to be deprived of His own, not by any Enemy, not even by ourselves. This is the last foundation of *Estel*, which we keep even when we contemplate the End: of all His designs the issue must be for His Children's joy. *Amdir* you have not, you say. Does no *Estel* at all abide?"

"Maybe," she said "But no! Do you not perceive that it is part of our wound that *Estel* should falter and its foundations be shaken? Are we the Children of the One? Are we not cast off finally? Or were we ever so? Is not the Nameless[2] the Lord of all the World?"

"Say is not even in question!" said Finrod.

"It cannot be unsaid," answered Andreth, "if you would understand the despair in which we walk. Or in which most Men walk. Among the Atani,[3] as you call us, or the Seekers as we say: those who left the lands of despair and the Men of darkness and journeyed west in vain hope: it is believed that healing may yet be found, or that there is some way of escape. But is this indeed *Estel?* Is it not *Amdir* rather; but without reason: mere flight in a dream from what waking they know: that there is no escape from darkness and death?"

"*Mere flight in a dream* you say," answered Finrod. "In dream many desires are revealed; and desire may be the last flicker of *Estel.* But you do not mean *dream*, Andreth. You confound *dream* and *waking* with *hope* and *belief*, to make the one more doubtful and the other more sure. Are they asleep when they speak of escape and healing?"

"Asleep or awake, they say nothing clearly," answered Andreth. "How or when shall healing come? To what manner of being shall those who see that time be re-made? And what of us who before it go out into darkness unhealed? To such questions only those of the "Old Hope" (as they call themselves) have any guess of an answer."

"*Those of the Old Hope?*" said Finrod. "Who are they?"

"A few," she said; "but their number has grown since we came to this land, and they see that the Nameless can (as they think) be defied. Yet that is no good reason. To defy him does not undo his work of old. And if the valour of the Eldar[4] fails here, then their despair will be deeper. For it was not on the might of Men, or of any of the peoples of Arda,[5] that the old hope was grounded."

"What then was this hope, if you know?" Finrod asked.

"They say," answered Andreth: "they say that the One will himself enter into Arda, and heal Men and all the Marring[6] from the beginning to the end. This they say also, or they feign, is a rumour that has come down through years uncounted, even from the days of our undoing."[7]

"They say, they feign?" said Finrod. "Are you then not one of them?"

"How can I be, lord? All wisdom is against them. Who is the One, whom ye call Eru? If we put aside the Men who serve the Nameless, as do many in Middle-earth, still many Men perceive the world only as a war between Light and Dark equipotent. But you will say: nay, that is Manwë[8] and Melkor; Eru is above them. Is then Eru the greatest of the Valar,[9] a great god among gods, as most Men will say, even among the Atani: a king who dwells far from his kingdom and leaves lesser princes to do here much as they will? Again you say: nay, Eru is One, alone without peer, and He made Eä,[10] and is beyond it; and the Valar are greater than we, but yet no nearer to His majesty. Is this not so?"

"Yes," said Finrod. "We say this, and the Valar we know, and they say the same, all save one. But which, think you, is more likely to lie: those who make themselves humble. Or he that exalts himself?"

"I do not doubt." said Andreth. "And for that reason the saying of Hope passes my understanding. How could Eru enter into the thing that he has made, and than which He is beyond measure greater? Can the singer enter into his tale or the designer into his picture?"

"He is already in it, as well as outside," said Finrod. "But indeed the 'in-dwelling' and the 'out-living' are not in the same mode."

"Truly," said Andreth. "So may Eru in that mode be present in Eä that proceeded from Him. But they speak of Eru Himself *entering in Arda,* and that is a thing wholly different. How could He the greater do this? Would it not shatter Arda, or indeed all Eä?"

"Ask me not," said Finrod. "These things are beyond the compass of the wisdom of the Eldar, or of the Valar maybe. But I doubt that our words may mislead us, and that when you say 'greater' you think of the dimensions of Arda, in which the greater vessel may not be contained in the less.

"But such words may not be used of the Measureless. If Eru wished to do this, I do not doubt that He would find a way, though I cannot foresee it. For, as it seems to me, even if He in Himself were to enter in, He must still remain also as He is: the Author without. And yet, Andreth, to speak with humility, I cannot conceive how else this healing could be achieved. Since Eru will surely not suffer Melkor to turn the world to his own ill and to triumph in the end. Yet there is no power conceivable greater than Melkor save Eru only. Therefore Eru, if He will not relinquish His work to Melkor, who must else proceed to mastery, then Eru must come in to conquer him.

"More: even if Melkor (or the Morgoth that he has become) could in any way be thrown down or thrust from Arda, still his Shadow would remain, and the evil that he has wrought and sown as a seed would wax and multiply. And if any remedy for this is to be found, ere all is ended, any new light to oppose the shadow, or any medicine for the wounds: then it must, I deem, come from without."

"Then, lord," said Andreth, and she looked up in wonder, "you believe in this Hope?"

"Ask me not yet," he answered. "For it is still to me but strange news that comes from afar. No such hope was ever spoken to the Quendi.[11] To you only it was sent. And yet through you we may hear it and lift up our hearts." He paused a while, and then looking gravely at Andreth he said: "Yes, Wise-woman, maybe it was ordained that we Quendi, and ye Atani, ere the world grows old, should meet and bring news one to another, and so we should learn of the Hope from you: ordained, indeed, that thou and I, Andreth, should sit here and speak together, across the gulf that divides our kindreds, so that while the Shadow still broods in the North we should not be wholly afraid."

Endnotes

1 "The One," "Eru," the "Father of All," or Ilúvatar—existing before and the maker of all through the Music of the Ainur.

2 That is, Melkor, or Morgoth, as the first Dark Lord was called throughout the First Age

3 The Elves call the race of Men *Atani*, literally meaning "Second People" (the Elves being the First).

4 The Elves, specifically the elves called "People of the Great Journey"

5 *Arda* is the World and all that is in it.

6 The Marring of Arda was due to the actions of Melkor

7 An event that occurred soon after Men awoke in the East at the first Sunrise. See Genesis 3

8 "Blessed One," greatest of the Valar and king of Arda

9 The fourteen powerful spirits who took physical form to enter Arda and fight the evils of Melkor

10 the whole universe

11 "Those who speak with voices"—when the first Elves awoke, they named themselves this since they thought that they were the only ones in Arda who were able to speak.

DISCUSSION QUESTIONS

1. What common heritage do elves and mankind share?
2. What is meant by the "Old Hope"? What theological terms might we use in our present age instead of the Old Hope?
3. What is meant by "the days of our undoing"?
4. What physical limitation does Andreth see that keeps her from being a believer in the promise of the Old Hope?

THE LORD OF THE RINGS
Project—The Philosophy of Tolkien

Following are a few questions based on The Philosophy of Tolkien *by Peter Kreeft, an excellent book to read after completing* The Lord of the Rings. *In the book Kreeft organizes the philosophical themes in* The Lord of the Rings *into 50 categories, accompanied by over 1,000 references to the text of the books.*

1. How does the magic of the elves differ from that of Sauron?

_____

_____

_____

_____

_____

2. If we define magic as the ability to control Nature for our own ends, then technology easily falls in the category of magic. How should this affect our approach toward technology?

_____

_____

_____

_____

_____

_____

3. Who could be viewed as Christ figures in *The Lord of the Rings* and why?

_____

_____

_____

_____

_____

THE LORD OF THE RINGS
Project—The Philosophy of Tolkien

4. In *The Lord of the Rings,* Middle Earth ("Midgard" as the Norse would say) is our Earth. It is the same planet we live on now, only as it is imagined to have existed many, many years ago. How does the setting of a real earth affect the way we perceive the story? How would it have been different if this Middle Earth was an alien planet?

_____

_____

_____

_____

5. How does the mythologizing of trees in the form of Ents make us see nature differently?

_____

_____

_____

_____

6. The Ring grants a sort of immortality to its bearer, an unnatural extension of his life through its power. How does Tolkein lead us to believe that death is preferable to this immortality? How might this apply to our lives in the modern world?

_____

_____

_____

_____

THE LORD OF THE RINGS
Answers

BOOK ONE
A Long-Expected Party
1. Bilbo and Frodo Baggins
2. Drogo was drowned, leaving Frodo an orphan.
3. Sam learned his letters—how to read.
4. fireworks—his skill with fires, smokes and lights
5. Hobbits give presents to other people on their own birthdays.
6. one gross—twelve dozen
7. Bilbo offered as the purpose of the party: to tell the guests how very fond he was of them all; to celebrate the birthdays of Frodo and himself; to announce that he was leaving—after which he vanished.
8. stretched
9. the ring
10. "my precious"
11. *Adelard Took:* umbrella/she took many of Bilbo's umbrellas
    Dora Baggins: waste basket/she wrote many letters of unwanted advice
    Milo Burrows: gold pen and ink bottle/Milo was poor at correspondence
    Angelica Baggins: mirror/she was vain
    Hugo Bracegirdle: empty bookcase/he borrowed many books without returning them
    Lobelia Sackville-Baggins: silver spoons/she had taken many of his good spoons years ago.
12. "Keep it safe, and keep it secret!"

The Shadows of the Past
1. celebrating Bilbo's birthday
2. Folco Boffin, Fredegar Bolger, Peregrin Took, and Meriadoc Brandybuck
3. Any of the following answers: the evil power driven out of Mirkwood by the White Council had reappeared in the Land of Mordor and had rebuilt the Dark Tower, Orcs were multiplying, cunning, well-armed Trolls were about and other evil creatures were hinted at.
4. a giant elm Tree-man walking
5. Saruman the White was chief of the wizard's order, head of the White Council and very learned in the lore of Elvenrings and the secret of their making.
6. Frodo saw fiery Elvish letters that, translated into the Common Tongue, read: "One Ring to rule them all, One Ring to find them, One Ring to bring them all and in the darkness bind them." It is the Master-ring.
7. If he recovered it, then he would command all the rings again, wherever they may be, even the Three elven rings, and all that had been made would be laid bare, and he would be stronger than ever.
8. His friend Aragorn, "the greatest traveller and huntsman of this age of the world."
9. Pity and Mercy
10. He sent Sam into exile with Frodo.

Three is Company
1. to the Sackville-Baggins
2. Gandalf
3. the beer-barrel in the cellar
4. a fox
5. ". . . great river: its springs were at every doorstep, and every path was its tributary."
6. a large man crouched in the saddle of a black horse, wrapped in a great black cloak and hood which only revealed his boots in the high stirrups
7. Woodhall
8. He had seen Bilbo twice—saying farewell to him on the spot they were now on and seeing him somewhere else.
9. ". . . for they are subtle and quick to anger."
10. ". . . for they will say both no and yes."

A Short Cut to Mushrooms and *A Conspiracy Unmasked*
1. Sam
2. Pippin (and Sam) did not want to miss out on the Golden Perch and "the best beer in the Eastfarthing"
3. As a youth Frodo had been caught by Old Maggot stealing the farmer's mushrooms and Maggot told his dogs to eat Frodo if he ever was in Bamfurlong again.
4. He told them about the visit he had had from a Black Rider.
5. a basket of mushrooms
6. They were fond of boats, and some could swim.
7. three tubs and a copper full of boiling water for baths
8. Merry told Frodo that they all knew he was planning on leaving the Shire at once, did not want to, and that they knew about the Ring.
9. Sam; ". . . take them as was willing"
10. Fredegar was to stay behind at Crickhollow to

THE LORD OF THE RINGS
Answers

keep up appearances as long as possible that Frodo was still living at the long, low turf-roofed house.

The Old Forest and *In the House of Tom Bombadil*

1. The most unfriendly trees will drop a branch, stick out a root or grasp at you with a long trailer.
2. They took a nap under a old, hoary willow-tree.
3. swallow them
4. Tom was a man-like person ("too large and heavy for a hobbit, if not quite tall enough for one of the Big People") clad in great yellow boots, a blue coat, and a battered hat sporting a long blue feather. His face was as red as an apple, creased with hundreds of laugh wrinkles and he had a long, brown beard.
5. a fair, yellow-haired young queen in a gown of silver-beaded green and a belt of gold and flowers
6. It was Goldberry's washing day and autumn-cleaning.
7. Tom told the hobbits about the Barrow-wights of the Barrow-downs and their history.
8. Farmer Maggot, because "There's earth under his old feet, and clay on his fingers; wisdom in his bones, and both his eyes are open."
9. It seemed to grow larger. None.
10. Keep to the green grass, avoid the Wights, and pass their barrows on the west-side if they strayed too near one.

Fog on the Barrow-Downs

1. They hadn't said farewell to the River's daughter, Goldberry.
2. They fell asleep.
3. A barrow-wight seized him.
4. a long, naked sword
5. He sang a rhyme—calling for Tom.
6. The hobbits were awakened.
7. the hobbit's ponies—Tom named them such
8. A blue brooch was chosen for Goldberry and Tom gave the hobbits leaf-shaped daggers decorated with weaving, serpentine knotwork in red and gold.
9. *The Prancing Pony*
10. hobbits and Big Folk

At the Sign of the Prancing Pony and *Strider*

1. they believed Rangers to have strange powers of sight and hearing/understood the languages of the animals
2. good food and excellent beer
3. writing a book about hobbits living outside the Shire
4. gray eyes, dark and shaggy hair flecked with gray, tall with high leather boots caked in mud, a travel-stained, heavy, dark cloak with a hood, and he smoked a long-stemmed, carved pipe
5. *Two answers would be acceptable:* "the little dog laughed to see such fun" or Frodo rolled off the table and disappeared
6. to travel with the hobbits until he wished to leave
7. a letter from Gandalf
8. Aragorn, son of Arathorn
9. The sword was broken a foot below the hilt.
10. the Black Breath

THE LORD OF THE RINGS
Answers

A Knife in the Dark
1. Fatty Bolger ran from the Black Riders, and his neighbor interpreted his babbling as a warning of enemies in Buckland—perhaps some strange invasion from the Old Forest.
2. Their ponies were missing, and they needed to find at least one pony to carry their supplies.
3. The five ponies that had been scared/driven off were sent down to Bree by Tom Bombadil, so Butterbur got five ponies at a very fair price.
4. hitting Bill Ferny in the nose
5. Amon Sûl, that is, Weathertop. Amon Sûl was where the largest and most powerful palantir in the North was kept during the Second Age.
6. The Black Riders could not see the world of light, but they saw shadows (except at noon) and perceived signs and forms in the dark, smelled the blood of living things, and the Ring drew them
7. Strider. "The Riders do not love it, and fear those who wield it."
8. Tinúviel rescued Beren from the dungeons of Sauron. One of the three Silmarils was use as the bride-price for the only daughter of King Thingol of Doriath.
9. He put on the Ring.
10. Elbereth/Gilthoniel. Both are names for Varda Elentári—the Queen of the Stars and spouse of Manwë the King of Arda.

Flight to the Ford
1. a black shadow
2. He threw the leaves from the plant (also known as Kingsfoil or asëa aranion) into boiling water and applied it to Frodo's wound.
3. a beryl
4. the trolls Tom, Bert and Bill Huggins
5. Glorfindel (of Rivendell, who fought at the Battle of Fornost)
6. Black Riders
7. The water rose, waves took on the form of white riders on white horses and swept the Black Riders away.

BOOK TWO

Many Meetings
1. Aragorn and an Elf-lord with flaming brands; Gandalf added the extra touch of the white horses and riders
2. "Lord of the Ring"/they should not name evil things—especially not the master of the Dark Tower of Mordor
3. Arwen Undómiel was a lady fair to look upon with dark hair and gray eyes, wearing a silver lace netted with glittering white gems on her head and a soft grey dress with a girdle of silver leaves.
4. Glóin, son of Gróin. He was one of the twelve companions of Thorin Oakenshield and Bilbo Baggins on the Quest of Erebor.
5. Bilbo
6. taking out the Ring to show Bilbo
7. Aragorn Elessar, Son of Arathorn—Strider. It was the singular form of *Dúnedain*, a term used for the Men of Númenor and their descendants.
8. mithril and elven glass
9. He made up verse about Eärendil in the house of Elrond.

The Council of Elrond
1. They went to Moria thirty years earlier and had not been heard from in a very long time.
2. Elrond
3. to seek counsel and ask for an explanation of the words dreamnt by Boromir's brother
4. the doubt of Boromir
5. the Ring; Isildur; Gandalf; the scrolls and books of Gondor; Denethor
6. that the One Ring was found, that it was long in the Shire, and that it is in Rivendell
7. Radagast the Brown—one of the five Wizards sent to Middle-earth in the Third Age. He was a master of shapes and changes of hue and was knowledgeable in the lore of animals and plants. He befriended beasts and was able to communicate with birds.
8. Saruman had "broken" white to become "Saruman of Many Colors."
9. Gwaihir the Windlord flew to his rescue.
10. the king of Rohan
11. Tom might take the Ring if all the free folk of the world begged him to, "but he would not understand the need" and might forget it or even

THE LORD OF THE RINGS
Answers

throw it away. "Such things have no hold on his mind."
12. Bilbo does not need to take the Ring back and finish the affair
13. he volunteered to take the Ring

The Ring Goes South
1. so there would be "some intelligence" in the party
2. Nine Walkers who were good to offset the evil Nine Riders
3. Sting and the mithril shirt that Thorin had given to him
4. Bill, the pony
5. snowed on them until they relented and turned around

A Journey in the Dark
1. through Moria/going via the Gap of Rohan would take the Ring Bearer too close to Isengard
2. *Fire be for saving of us! Fire against the werewolf-host!* The tree above Gandalf burst into flame and the fire leaped from tree-top to tree-top, crowning the hill in dazzling light.
3. The Sirannon had been dammed and had filled the valley.
4. *Speak, friend, and enter*
5. The Watcher in the Water (a beast with tentacles that could reach out possibly thirty feet—perhaps a kraken) shut them and uprooted the trees that grew on either side, barring the doors.
6. Gandalf
7. Gandalf suggests that Pippin throw himself in
8. the right-hand passage did not smell as bad as left-hand passage
9. It was worth more than the entire Shire and everything in it.
10. Balin, son of Fundin, Lord of Moria—he and his younger brother, Dwalin, were among the dwarves that traveled with Bilbo in the Quest of Erebor.

The Bridge of Khazad-dûm
1. the Book of Mazarbul/Balin died on November 10th from an Orc arrow received in Dimrill Dale —a valley lying east of Khazad-dûm (also called *Nanduhirion* in Sindarin)
2. Frodo stabbed the cave-troll in the foot with Sting
3. cast a shutting-spell on the door

4. Seeing Durin's Bane, the Balrog. A Balrog is a demon that was originally *maiar,* like Sauron, Saruman and Gandalf, that was seduced by Morgoth and corrupted before the making of Arda.
5. The Balrog swung his whip and caught Gandalf, dragging him down into the abyss. "Fly, you fools!" were Gandalf's last words.

Lothlórien
1. In Kheled-zâram, also called Mirrormere, they saw the crown of Durin—glinting stars in the deep water.
2. He discovered Frodo's mithril-coat.
3. he thought he heard the quick patter of feet and saw two gleams of light behind them—and had since they first entered Moria
4. Legolas told him that the elves said that they could shoot him in the dark because he breathed so loudly.
5. the dwarf/blindfolded
6. Two ropes were stretched across, and they walked on one and held on to the other for balance. The Celebrant river begins in the eastern Misty Mountains and runs through Lórien to where it meets the Nimrodel river.
7. He ordered that they all be blindfolded.
8. The Company were allowed to remove their blindfolds at the mound of Amroth which stands in the heart of Lórien.
9. Frodo came across Aragorn saying "Fair Arwen [lit. Arwen your beauty], farewell!"

The Mirror of Galadriel
1. They arrived at the northern end of the city and Caras Galadhon only had gates on the southern end of the city.
2. They would stand.
3. the chance of flying home to the Shire to have a nice little hole and a bit of garden for his own
4. Gimli
5. a stanza about his fireworks
6. his home had been dug up, his father was alone, and the Shire crassly industrialized
7. Galadriel
8. Frodo offered the Ring to Galadriel, and she resisted the offer.
9. To Sam, Nenya looked like a star through Galadriel's finger.

THE LORD OF THE RINGS
Answers

Project—Truth and Poetry
What is it about poetry that makes something more real or validates something, making it more true?
Ken Myers (www.MarsHillAudio.org) commented on this idea to the author of this guide, and following are some excerpts of his thoughts on the topic:

Could it be that, created by the Word, the World is in its depth ordered as language? And that we know the World best when we speak of it with language engaged in its greatest intensity, with assonance and rhythm and allusion and metaphor?

... Poetic expression conveys a heightened sense of reality because it relies on the connectedness that is the fabric of reality. In Tom Howard's *Chance or the Dance* he says: "Imagination is, in a word, the faculty by which we organize the content of our experience into some form, and thus apprehend it as significant. Put another way, it is what makes us refuse to accept experience as mere random clutter, and makes us try without ceasing to shape that experience so that we can manage it." One of the outlets for imagination is metaphor. Simple metaphors explain experience in an imaginative and connected way that dozens of other words cannot. Furthermore, imagination gives concreteness to vague or elusive things. It compares the significance of one thing (a frown) to the significance of another (a thundercloud). We are creatures who seek to understand and express significance in our experiences, Howard says.

Poetry is the rhythmic language which imposes a form on our experience. Howard continues his analysis of rhythm by saying, "I should think there are at least four kinds of satisfaction aroused by rhythm: the satisfactions of resolution, of recurrence, of recognition, and of transfiguration...." Really, he proposes, our lives are based on rhythm and the poet merely gives connectedness and significance to ordinary experience. Poetry "addresses our imagination and ... it tries to beguile us into an intense awareness of our experience".

... Educator James Taylor (not balladeer James Taylor) in a book called *Poetic Knowledge* asserts that in order to have knowlegde of the world that is engaged with the world that participates in the reality of the world, it must be subjective knowledge. Poetry moves us in that direction. Here, Taylor is relying a lot on Jacques Maritain's argument in *Creative Intuition in Art and Poetry*. Taylor writes: "... truth that is subjective is truth that one has made one's own—the observer is now engaged in the thing through connatural knowledge, and one has, through sympathy, participated in the reality (albeit obscurely) of the experience, so that knowledge ceases to be mere information and becomes existential and recalled as real. Poetic experience leading to poetic knowledge is concerned 'with bringing men into engagement with what is true. What is important is engagement with reality, not simply the discerning of reality.'"

Timeline Project
1. Frodo
4. Boromir
20. Saruman
19. Edoras
23. Shadowfax
25. Crickhollow
26. Tom Bombadil
28. Barrow-wight
29. Gaffer
30. Bree
3. Weathertop
6. Frodo
13. Bridge
18. Glorfindel
24. Boromir
25. Elrond
11. snow
13. Moria
17. Company

Farewell to Lórien and *The Great River*
1. boats
2. in addition to the boats, the lembas, elven cloaks with leaf broochs, at their final meal together the Lord and Lady of Galadhrim gave Aragorn a sheath for Andúril, and also the Elessar (a great emerald-green stone, set in a silver brooch in the form of an eagle with outspread wings), Boromir a golden belt, Merry and Pippin small silver belts, Legolas a Galadhrim bow strung with elf hair and arrows, Sam a small gray wooden box with earth from Galadriel's orchard (a gift which proved very valuable in the revival of the Shire after the desolation of Saurman—the box also contained a

THE LORD OF THE RINGS
Answers

silver nut, that turned out to be from a Mallorn tree, the last east of the sea), Gimli was given three strands of Galadriel's hair, a boon that not even Fëanor was granted before, and to Frodo the Phial of Galadriel—to light his way in the dark places of the world, and to comfort him against the pains that plagued his later years.
3. the danger of light and joy
4. He thought he saw a log with eyes and decided that it was Gollum.
5. They were attacked by Orcs' arrows and a great, dark winged creature that Legolas shot.
6. It seemed to Sam that it was in its wrong phase, due to him losing track of time while in Caras Galadon.
7. Also known as The Gates of Argonath, the Pillars of the Kings are two enormous pillars, carved in the likenesses of Isildur and Anárion, standing upon either side of the River Anduin. Each of the two figures wears a crown and a helm, with an axe in its right hand and its left hand raised in a gesture of defiance to the enemies of Gondor.

The Breaking of the Fellowship
1. Orcs were near.
2. Boromir found him and tried to talk him into letting Boromir borrow the Ring.
3. Sam, Gimli and Aragorn would go with Frodo and the rest of the Company would go to Minas Tirith.
4. Sam thought Frodo was screwing up his courage to go off to Mount Doom alone.
5. Sam jumped in after the boat Frodo was in and nearly drowned.

Project
1. In the book it was a combined birthday party for Bilbo and Frodo. In the movie the party was just for Bilbo.
2. The journey was drastically cut, making the viewer feel like it took a much shorter time, as well as skipping important events like their visit with Tom Bombadil, visit to Farmer Maggot's, acquiring Bill the Pony, and making the inclusion of Merry and Pippin in their travels appear to be an accident rather than a demonstration of loyalty.
3. Arwen Evenstar
4. 12 years

BOOK THREE
The Departure of Boromir
and The Riders of Rohan
1. Boromir sitting against a tree pierced with many arrows, his horn cloven, his sword broken near the hilt and dead Orcs piled all around him and at his feet.
2. The Orcs bound the halflings and took them alive, but whether or not the Ring-bearer was with them, Boromir did not say.
3. a small white hand on a black field
4. They laid him in one of the boats, with an elven cloak beneath his head, the gold belt of Lorien around his waist, his cloven horn and sword on his lap, and the weapons of his enemies beneath his feet.
5. chase the Orcs to retrieve Merry and Pippin
6. five dead northern Orcs
7. Aragorn found footprints of Pippin and the brooch of his elven-cloak, so they knew at least Pippin was alive.
8. proud and wilful, true-hearted, generous, bold, wise, unlearned, singers of songs
9. Gimli was upset that Éomer insulted Galadriel.
10. Legolas drew his bow, promising to kill Éomer before he had finished decapitating Gimli.
11. He laughed and said that hobbits were only little people out of legend and children's tales.
12. because they traveled 45 leagues in four days
13. that they return the horses to Meduseld when their quest is achieved
14. They lost their horses and saw a mysterious, old man with a wide-brimmed hat and a great cloak, leaning on a staff

The Uruk-Hai
1. Boromir leaning against a tree, plucking out an arrow
2. Kill all but NOT the Halflings; they are to brought back ALIVE as quickly as possible.
3. cut the cords around his wrists and retie them in a loose bracelet
4. Grishnákh was present at the torture and interrogation of Gollum so he knew about the Ring and suspected Merry and Pippin might have it after hearing them imitate Gollum's trademark throat noise. Grishnákh tried to steal the hobbits away from the Uruk-hai in order to take them for himself but was killed by a Rider.
5. They ate some lembas.

THE LORD OF THE RINGS
Answers

Treebeard

1. It wasn't dark and black but rather dim and stuffy.
2. On top of the *a-lalla-lalla-rumba-kamanda-lind-or-burúmë* (the hill) was an Ent. Treebeard (or Fanghorn) was over fourteen feet tall with a man-like or troll-like figure with a bushy and twiggy beard. His skin was smooth brown, he had seven-toed feet and was covered in a green-grey bark-like hide. Humphrey Carpenter, in *J.R.R. Tolkien: A Biography,* writes that Tolkien:
   "began to sketch the episode where two of the hobbits encounter Treebeard, the being who was the ultimate expression of Tolkien's love and respect for trees. When eventually he came to write this chapter (so he told Nevill Coghill) he modeled Treebeard's way of speaking, *'Hrum, Hroom,'* on the booming voice of C.S. Lewis."
3. Ents were tree-herds.
4. Beginning at their toes, it rose bringing refreshment and vigour up to the tips of the hair.
5. Treebeard thought that the Entwives would like the Shire.
6. Saruman
7. The Entwives moved away from the Ents because they liked to plant and control things, so they moved across the Great River Anduin.
   This area was destroyed by Sauron, and the Entwives disappeared. The Ents looked for them but never found them. It is sung by the Ents that one day they will find each other. Sam mentions his cousin Hal claims to have seen a tree-like giant in the north of the Shire and Treebeard says the Entwives would like that land, leading some to hope that the Entwives may live near the Shire. Sadly, Tolkien wrote in letter #144 of *The Letters of J.R.R. Tolkien:* "I think that in fact the Entwives have disappeared for good, being destroyed with their gardens in the War of the Last Alliance . . ."
8. Bregalad got his nickname, Quickbeam, when he answered an elder Ent before that Ent had finished his question.
9. the wanton cutting down of trees—without even the bad excuse of feeding fires

The White Rider

1. The horses did not sound afraid but rather glad.
2. He found a mallorn-leaf and lembas crumbs.
3. Treebeard's Hill; he was now Gandalf the White
4. In the end he was able to sacrifice himself like the good and noble man that he truly was—aside from how he behaved while under the influence of the Ring.
5. "they choose the wisest person present to speak to" since "the long explanations needed by the young are wearying."
6. Sauron thought they were planning on taking the Ring to Minas Tirith to give to a warrior to wield in war against him. It hadn't crossed his mind that the Company actually intended to destroy the Ring.
7. Treebeard
8. They took the Endless Stair.
9. He thought he wasn't sent a message from Galadriel and then was overjoyed when she sent greeting to the Lockbearer and said her thoughts were with him and that he should "have a care to lay thine axe to the right tree."
10. They and the Ents had reached Isengard and were attacking it.

The King of the Golden Hall

1. weapons/the staff of Gandalf
2. *Láthspell:* "Ill-news"
3. With a flash of light, Gandalf struck him motionless.
4. locked in Wormtongue's chest
5. his pick of the treasure of Rohan and the hand of Éowyn
6. ride into battle to prove he is true to the king or to go (to Saruman)
7. Éowyn

Helm's Deep

1. "Ride to Helm's Deep! Go not to the Fords of Isen, and do not tarry in the plain!"
2. The swords Gúthwinë (Battle Friend) and Andúril (Flame of the West) were carried by Éomer and Aragorn through a small postern-door that opened in an angle of the burg-wall on the west. A small path ran from it around to the great gate.
3. Gimli beheaded two Orcs that had played opossum, tripped Éomer, and attacked him.

4. 21
5. The Orcs blasted a whole in the Deeping Wall where the drain had been.
6. Théoden, Aragorn and the lords of the House of Eorl the Young rode out and sent the enemy running back towards the Dike.
7. the arrival of Gandalf and Erkenbrand, lord of the Westfold, leading the Riders of the Rohirrim

Project

ERED NIMRAIS

Glittering Caves

N

Rear Gate

ERED NIMRAIS

The Hornburg

Deeping Wall

Outer Court

Inner Court

Postern Door

Great Gate

Helm's Dike

DEEPING STREAM

The Road to Isengard

1. Gimli=42, Legolas=41
2. the trees attacking the Orcs
3. They had not expected mercy—Saruman had told them that the men of Rohan were cruel and burned their captives.
4. They agreed that if they come safely through all that lies ahead of them, Gimli would visit Fanghorn with Legolas and Legolas would see Helm's Deep with Gimli.
5. Legolas saw eyes looking out of the shadows, and Théoden and the rest of the company got to see three Ents.
6. A huge pit a mile below the Dike that had stones piled into a hill. In the middle of the night the Huorns had buried the Orcs there.
7. The great circular wall of the Ring of Isengard came out of the arm of the mountain, was made of black stone, and was one mile across. There

was a single entrance—an arched tunnel bored through the south side, with gates made of iron that swung easily and noiselessly on their steel hinges. Around the inner side of the Ring of Isengard, there were many rooms and halls carved into the great wall with dens beneath the walls where wolves were kept. Within the Ring of Isengard was a plain and at the center stood the gleaming black Tower of Orthanc. The Tower rose to a height of 500 feet and then forked into four sharp pinnacles, with a small roof of polished stone carved with astronomical signs.

In the early days of Isengard, there were gardens and groves of trees on the plain, but Saruman had had these destroyed. The paths were paved and lined with pillars linked by chains. Deep shafts were dug into the plain, containing store-rooms, armories, and smithies. In *Ents, Elves and Eriador: The Environmental Vision of J.R.R. Tolkien,* Matthew Dickerson and Jonathan Evans write: "Saruman's actions constitute two kinds of evil: deforestation for utilitarian purposes and destruction of forests simply to let them rot. This is what we can expect from the likes of Saruman. A bad steward of his own land will probably be a bad steward of other people's, and the ill effects are bound to spill over into the surrounding landscape."

Tolkien also shows us Saruman's evil—in particular, the evil of his anti-ecology—in the manner in which he does battle . . . "a very tall handsome Ent, got caught in a spray of some liquid fire and burned like a torch: a horrible sight." Saruman, it seems, has used some sort of defoliating agent or other form of chemical warfare. Besides showing that he considers the trees and their guardians his enemies, this shows us that his war on Rohan is also a war against the land itself.

8. Meriadoc, son of Saradoc, and Peregrin, son of Paladin—Merry was smoking, and Pippin was napping.
9. Having to listen to a lengthy discussion of herblore and the history of the practice of pipe smoking among the *holbytlan.*
10. the water, Quickbeam, and some other Ents

THE LORD OF THE RINGS
Answers

Flotsam and Jetsam

1. The hobbits appeared taller and their hair curlier and thicker.
2. a small pipe
3. nine
4. Aragorn returned to the hobbits their Westernesse blades and Pippin's Elven brooch. Merry explained the sword's effect onthe Uruk-Hai: "At first I thought he was going to stab me, but he threw the things away as if they burned him."
5. Merry Brandybuck thought that Huorns were Ents that had become more like trees. And Treebeard had spoken of trees that had become Entish, so it is possible that some of these were Huorns. Regardless, they were wild and queer, looking like trees with twisted roots and long, grasping branches. They were hard to see move, since they seemed to be wrapped in shadow. Fangorn Forest was the home of many Huorns where they generally just stood at rest, keeping watch over ordinary trees.
6. He was sprayed with liquid fire and burned like a torch.
7. "Get up, you tom-fool of a Took!"
8. They diverted the Isen, and with it flooded Isengard.
9. Wormtongue
10. Aragorn was puzzled by the presence of Southfarthing leaf in Isengard—and from the 1417 crop.

The Voice of Saruman and The Palantír

1. "Beware of his voice!"
2. when Saruman was hanging from a gibbet at a window in Othanac for the crows to have sport with
3. king's jester
4. surrender of the key to the tower of Orthanc and his staff
5. Saruman's staff
6. to allow Legolas to bring Gimli into Fanghorn to visit and explore the woods
7. stealing the seeing stone and looking into it—which allowed Sauron to question the hobbit, almost to the ruin of them all
8. Aragorn
9. They were made by the Elves of Valinor in the Uttermost West, almost certainly by the Noldor and possibly by Fëanor.
10. Minas Tirith—"before the seas of war surround it"

BOOK FOUR
The Taming of Sméagol and The Passage of the Marshes

1. a bit of bread and half a mug of beer
2. elvish rope
3. The rope came down. Frodo thought it was due to a faulty knot, and Sam thought it was because he had called it.
4. Frodo remembered Gandalf's words of pity and mercy for Gollum.
5. Gollum says that Sméagol will swear on the Precious to "never, to let Him have it" and to "serve the master of the Precious."
6. Fish. This was the riddle Bilbo solved before he found the Ring.
7. He thinks the elf food tastes like "dust and ashes."
8. Frodo did not think they would survive their job of destroying the Ring.
9. In the pools in the middle of the marshes, the faces of the dead could still be seen by flickering lights—candles of corpses. The Dead Marshes were the graves of the Elves, Men, and Orcs who had died in a battle on the plain of Dagorlad during the War of the Last Alliance in 3434 of the Second Age.
10. A nazgûl on a fell beast flew overhead, "across the moon, and with a deadly cry went away westward, out running the wind in its fell speed." At this time the Ents were attacking Isengard and the battle of Helm's Deep would soon begin.
11. Sméagol promised to help *the master of the Precious,* but if Gollum took the Ring, then *he'd* be the master of the Precious and wouldn't need to obey the hobbits anymore.
12. "Eat fish every day, three times a day, fresh from the sea."

The Black Gate is Closed and Of Herbs and Stewed Rabbit

1. the Men of Gondor—to keep Sauron out
2. give the Ring to Sméagol for safe keeping
3. "I should put on the Precious;" and command Sméagol and he would obey, even if the order was "to leap from a precipice or to cast yourself in the fire."
4. The Silent Watchers. These mysterious beings are never clearly identified, but it appears that they were the triple-bodied (one guarding the way into the tower, one the way out, and the third

staring across the gateway), vulture-headed creatures with eyes of black stone that sat within the archway of the Tower's gate.
5. rabbits
6. Sam stewed the rabbits
7. Faramir, Boromir's brother
8. In battle, the oliphaunts carried ornate red and gold tower-like structures on their backs.

The Window on the West
1. Isildur's Bane
2. Frodo learned of Boromir's death—that it was not a vision sent by the Enemy, for the two halves of his horn rested now on Denethor's lap.
3. Gandalf
4. None. Faramir said, "I would not take this thing, if it lay by the highway. Not were Minas Tirith falling in ruin and I alone could save her . . ."
5. They stood in silence for a moment, facing west "towards Numenor that was, and beyond to Elvenhome that is, and to that which is beyond Elvenhome and will ever be."
6. Frodo steered clear of matters concerning the Ring and played up Boromir's valiance in their adventures.
7. Faramir said that the decline of Gondor's civilization was because of the Numenoreans' hunger for/pursuit of everlasting life, internal fighting and giving themselves "over wholly to idleness and ease."
8. Galadriel
9. He mentioned the Ring.
10. Sam said that Faramir showed he was of the very highest quality and that the captain reminded him of Gandalf.

The Forbidden Pool and Journey to the Cross-Roads
1. to protect Gollum from Faramir killing him
2. Faramir thought Gollum was wicked, malice ate at him like a canker, and that he was leading Frodo into a place where a dark terror dwelled.
3. In addition to some food, Faramir gave the hobbits carved and reshod staves made of *lebethron*.
4. decapitated it and put a rock in place bearing a grin and one red eye.
5. The king's head was crowned again—the stone statue's head had a crown of flowers.

The Stairs of Cirith Ungol and Shelob's Lair
1. He felt compelled to run up the gleaming road towards its gate.
2. the phial of Galadriel
3. the Winding Stair
4. Beren went into Thangorodrim to steal a Silmaril from Morgoth's crown in the First Age, and that jewel became the Star of Earendil. The light of that Star was contained in the phial of Galadriel, which Frodo carried.
5. Sam tried to ask Gollum if he'd like to be the hero in their story.
6. sneaking
7. Shelob running from Sting and the phial of Galadriel
8. Orc slaves. Shelob was the last child of Ungoliant, the Maiar spirit who helped Melkor (Morgoth) destroy the two trees of Valinor.
9. fighting Gollum—Sam broke it over Gollum's back

The Choices of Master Samwise
1. Shelob had Frodo wrapped from ankle to shoulder
2. Seeking to crush Sam, accidentally Shelob thrust herself onto Sting.
3. He filled her mind with inner lightnings sprung from the blazing phial of Galadriel.
4. Sting, the phial and the Ring. Sam did not take the mithril coat.
5. Sam was able to understand the speech of Orcs.
6. Frodo was not dead.
7. a great big elvish warrior
8. a bolted iron gate

Project
1. He declares that he has no desire for it, saying he wouldn't take it even if he found it by the side of a road.
2. the forbidden pool.
3. Orcs mounted on wargs attack the Rohirrim, resulting in Aragorn's near death—he is revived by a vision of Arwen in a dream sequence.
4. Arwen has a vision of her future, which is loosely based on "The Tale of Aragorn and Arwen" in the appendices.
5. Old Man Willow appears in Fangorn Forest and is pacified by Treebeard (in the extended version).
6. In the movie, the Ent is unaware of what is happening on the borders of his forest and has to be "tricked" into attacking Isengard.

The Lord of the Rings
Answers

Book Five
Minas Tirith

1. the beacons of Gondor
2. "... a vast pier of rock whose huge out-thrust bulk divided in two all the circles of the City save the first. ... its edge sharp as a ship-keel facing east. Up it rose, even to the level of the topmost circle, and there was crowned by a battlement; so that those in the Citadel might, like mariners in a moutainous ship, look from its peak sheer down upon the Gate seven hundred feet below."
3. Denethor was proud and subtle. It was not wise to bring news of the death of Boromir while also speaking of one who would claim kingship over Denethor.
4. Faramir
5. his fealty and service to Gondor
6. Boromir did not lead the Company from Moria and that there was one of high honor who had a famous sword. Denethor intentionally slighted Gandalf by having him not speak—to remind Gandalf that he ruled Gondor and not the wizard.
7. Beregond son of Baranor; when and where could he get something to eat?
8. It was the chief city of Gondor before it was ruined by the forces of Mordor. Boromir led his army against the Orcs and took it back for Gondor.
9. Beregond's son, Bergil
10. Gandalf said he would take Pippin when the summons came, because there would be no dawn—the Darkness had begun.

Project—Diagram of Minas Tirith
It was built on seven levels, each delved into the hill, and about each was set a wall, and in each wall a gate. But the gates were not set in a line: the Great Gate in the City Wall was at the east point of the circuit, but the next faced half south, and the third half north, and so to and fro upwards; so that the paved way that climbed towards the Citadel turned first this way and then that across the face of the hill. And each time that it passed the line of the Great Gate it went through an arched tunnel, piercing a vast pier of rock whose huge out-thrust bulk divided in two all the circles of the City save the first.

P 1.   Embrasure
D 2.   White Tree
L 3.   Fen Hollen
Q 4.   Great Gate
J 5.   The Hallows
B 6.   King's House
O 7.   Old Guesthouse
G 8.   Mount Mindolluin
M 9.   House of Healing
N 10. Othram (City Wall)
I 11. House of the Stewards
K 12. Rath Dinen (Silent Street)
H 13. House of the Kings
F 14. Place of the Fountain
D 15. White Tower of Ecthelion
A 16. Gandalf and Pippen's Room
C 17. Merethrond (Great Hall of Feast)

The Passing of the Grey Company

1. Halbarad and twenty-nine other Dunadain, along with Elrond's two sons—Elladan and Elrohir.
2. "The days are short. If thou art in haste, remember the Paths of the Dead."
3. Meriadoc of the Shire
4. He looked in the Seeing Stone and decided to follow the Paths of the Dead.
5. Isildur cursed them and said that they would never rest until they fulfilled their oath to fight Sauron. The King and his Men then hid, and over time they died, but their spirits continued to haunt the mountains.
6. Aragorn
7. a cage
8. Gimli
9. follow Aragorn to Pelargir and when the land is clean of the servants of Sauron then the oath would be fulfilled.
10. No device was seen on the standard—it appeared to be black, the heraldric elements (the White Tree of Gondor and the Seven Stars and Crown of the King) being hidden in the darkness.

The Muster of Rohan

1. not to go to war
2. Merry saw them when he came to Dunharrow with King Théoden on March 9, 3019. The Púkelmen were carved of stone in the image of short, squat Men sitting cross-legged with their arms folded across their round bellies. The weathered statues stood at each turning of the zig-zag path leading up to the stronghold in the valley of Harrowdale in the White Mountains.

3. Baldor, the second king of Rohan, made an oath to enter the Paths of the Dead at the feast to celebrate the construction of Meduseld. His remains were discovered by Aragorn when he travelled through the Paths of the Dead. Baldor's mail-clad skeleton was found next to a stone door bearing marks of his fingers upon it. Years after the publishing of *The Lord of the Rings,* Tolkien's explanation of this incident was found in a linguistic journal called *Vinyar Tengwar:* "The special horror of the closed door before which the skeleton of Baldor was found was probably due to the fact that the door was the entrance to an evil temple hall [of the same Men of Darkness to which the Oathbreakers presumably belonged] to which Baldor had come, probably without opposition up to that point. But the door was shut in his face, and enemies that had followed him silently came up and broke his legs and left him to die in the darkness, unable to find any way out."
4. a single arrow, black feathered and barbed with steel but the point painted red
5. released Merry from his service
6. Dernhelm (which means "helmet of secrecy")

The Seige of Gondor
1. waiting hungry on others while they eat
2. Black Riders on fell beasts, flying across Pelennor Field. The White Rider keeps the Nazgul at bay with a white shaft of light that emanates from his outstretched hand.
3. Boromir would have brought his father a mighty gift—the Ring.
4. Gollum. Gollum leading Frodo to Cirith Ungol.
5. Denethor insists that Faramir go to the defense of Osgiliath.
6. Prince Imrahil
7. the heads of those that had fallen at Osgiliath, on the Rammas, or in the fields—branded with the mark of the Lidless Eye
8. Pippin refused to be released from Denethor's service
9. The Closed Door—Fen Hollen—led down to the Hallows, where the rulers of Gondor were entombed in the House of the Kings and the House of the Stewards in the Silent Street. It was only unlocked when there was a funeral.
10. between following orders and saving the life of Faramir
11. Grond was a battering ram 100 feet long with a head made of black steel shaped like a ravening wolf. It was hung from large war machines, pulled by Great Beasts and swung by Mountain-trolls against the iron doors of the City.
12. The Lord of the Nazgul had "a kingly crown; and yet upon no head visible was it set. The red fires shone between it and the mantled shoulders vast and dark. From a mouth unseen there came a deadly laughter." Gandalf barred the way, astride Shadowfax.
13. horns; the arrival of Rohan

The Ride of Rohirrim and *The Battle of the Pelennor Fields*
1. the Woses—Wild Men of the Wood
2. "... a strange squat shape of a man, gnarled as on old stone, and the hairs of his scanty beard straggled on his lumpy chin like dry moss. He was short-legged and fat-armed, thick and stumpy, and clad only with the grass about his waist."
3. If the people of Rohan live after their battle with Sauron, they must promise to leave the Woses alone and not hunt them in the woods like beasts.
4. He received word that the bodies of Hirgon (the messenger who had brought the Red Arrow of Gondor to Théoden) and another man of Gondor had been found, killed by Orcs.
5. They sang.
6. Dernhelm is "no man"—but instead, a woman.
7. Merry sneaked up behind him, and using his Westernesse blade that he got from the Barrow-wight, he cut the Witch-King behind the knee. Then Éowyn drove her sword between the crown and mantle, destroying the Witch-King.
8. His horse, Snowmane, fell upon him.
9. He noticed that she was not dead, as the Rohirrim had assumed, and encouraged them to rush her to the city for healing.
10. He saw Aragorn's standard—the White Tree of Gondor and the seven stars and the crown of Elendil on a black field—break on the foremost ship.

The Pyre of Denethor and *The Houses of Healing*
1. Through a palantír, confirming Gandalf's suspicion that the seeing stone of Minas Anor (the original name of Minas Tirith) had not been lost, but had been hidden in the Tower.

THE LORD OF THE RINGS
Answers

2. Denethor burned to death lying on a table, clasping a palantír. And he died alone, because Gandalf had taken Faramir.
3. Gandalf was in the sixth circle at the main door to the Houses of Healing.
4. bury him
5. Aragorn. He took the title because he thought it was unwise to take the title of king at that time, for fear that doubt and debate would distract them while Mordor was still a looming threat.
6. Gandalf was acting on a comment by Ioreth the wise-woman of Gondor: "The hands of the king are the hands of a healer, and so shall the rightful king be known."
7. Elrond. Aragorn traced his blood line back to Elrond's brother, Elros. Like Elrond, Elros was half-elven, but he had chosen to be mortal and from him the race of Numenoreans was descended.
8. *Athelas,* also known as *Kingsfoil* or *Asëa Aranion*
9. knight him
10. Merry said he would never smoke again since Théoden had died without them having chance to talk of herb-lore to the King as they had planned, so he wouldn't be able to smoke again without feeling the sadness of his loss. Aragorn told Merry to smoke and to think on the memory of his service to Théoden.
11. Elfstone

Project—Tower Times
Why call your newspaper "Tower Times" and not "Tirith Tribune" or "Gondor Gazette?" Minas Tirith—literally Tower of Guard—was originally Minas Anor—Tower of the Setting Sun. Originally the tower of Anárion the son of Elendil, it was renamed a thousand years before the War of the Ring.

The Last Debate and *The Black Gate Opens*
1. Legolas would bring people of the Wood to plant trees and provide birds for the city, while Gimli would bring stonewrights to fix and improve on the architecture.
2. An accounting of their trip on the Paths of the Dead.
3. "Pale swords were drawn; but I know not whether their blades would still bite, for the Dead needed no longer any weapon but fear. None would withstand them." Aragorn commanded the Shadow Host and then fell on the men of Umbar, driving them mad with fear. Many leapt overboard and drowned while the rest fled south, back towards their own lands.
4. stay and strengthen their strong places or march to certain defeat
5. because whoever had the Ring could not learn how to wield its full power quickly
6. The goal was to encourage Sauron to empty his lands and focus all his attention on creating a trap for the one he perceived to be the new Ringlord so that the Ring-bearer could go to destroy the Ring.
7. Merry
8. Gandalf suggested that they not take the Pass of Cirith Ungol to enter Mordor because of a great evil that lurked there. Also, if Frodo had gone that way, it was crucial that they didn't draw the attention of the Eye there.
9. "The King Elessar comes!"
10. Aragorn commanded them to re-take Cair Andros if they could and hold it.
11. Sam's sword, an Elven cloak with a brooch from Lorien and the mithril-mail that Frodo wore.
12. The Lieutenant of Barad-dûr revealed that Sauron did not have the Ring (or he wouldn't be bothering to parley) and that he did not know that there were *two* hobbits. If it was true that Frodo had been captured, the hope still existed that Sam might have the Ring and was continuing the Quest.
13. eagles

Project—Timeline
14. Galadriel
17. Gwaihir
25. Argonath
26. Boromir
29. Treebeard
30. Entmoot
1. Gandalf (the White)
2. Isengard
5. Minas Tirith
6. Merry
7. Faramir
8. Paths of the Dead
10. Morgul
12. Shelob's
13. orcs
15. Pelennor
18. Merry

THE LORD OF THE RINGS
Answers

BOOK SIX
The Tower of Cirith Ungol
1. lying outside the undergate of the Orcs' stronghold
2. His hearing was sharpened.
3. It was not made to keep enemies out of Mordor, but to keep them in—Men of Westernesse kept watch on the evil land of Sauron where his creatures still lurked. After his return to Mordor, Sauron found it useful because he had few servants but many slaves, so the tower retained its chief purpose of preventing escape from Mordor.
4. love for Frodo and plain hobbit-sense
5. Sam used the phial of Galadriel and its light to break the spell of the Watchers.
6. He sang.
7. thief
8. that they eat some lembas bread

The Land of the Shadow
1. the offer of a glass of water
2. light and water
3. Above the Mountains of Shadow Sam saw a star.
4. that the Orcs were looking for who had escaped the Tower and also that Gollum was nearby
5. He caught a glimpse of a black form or shadow flitting among the rocks near Frodo's hiding-place that was Gollum.
6. Slave-drivers saw them and ordered them to fall into line.
7. Other columns of Orcs arrived and as the different marching lines merged together, the hobbits fell to the ground and crawled to the edge of the road, diving into a shallow pit to hide.

Mount Doom
1. Sam thought that it would take Frodo at least a week to walk the fifty miles to reach the volcano.
2. "... as hope died in Sam, or seemed to die, it was turned to a new strength. Sam's plain hobbit-face grew stern, almost grim, as the will hardened in him, and he felt through his limbs a thrill ..."
3. his cooking gear
4. Sam carried Frodo
5. Barad-dûr—Sauron's Dark Tower
6. Gollum
7. "If you touch me ever again, you shall be cast yourself into the Fire of Doom."
8. killing Gollum

9. Gollum violently knocked Sam to the stony floor and Sauron suddenly bent his whole mind and purpose with overwhelming force upon the Mountain. "At his summons, wheeling with a rending cry, in a last desperate race there flew, faster than the winds, the Nazgul, the Ringwraiths, and with a storm of wings they hurtled southwards to Mount Doom."
10. Gollum bit it off of Frodo's finger.

The Field of Cormallen
1. The Towers of the Teeth collapsed and the Black Gate was hurled in ruin. "And as the Captains gazed south to the Land of Mordor, it seemed to them that, black against the pall of cloud, there rose a huge shape of shadow, impenetrable, lightning-crowned, filling all the sky. Enormous it reared above the world, and stretched out towards them a vast threatening hand, terrible but impotent: for even as it leaned over them, a great wind took it, and it was all blown away, and passed; and then a hush fell."
2. A *eucatastrophe* is the opposite of a catastrophe (the prefix *eu* is Greek for "good"). Gandalf, Gwaihir and the other eagles fly to look for Frodo and Sam.
3. Sam cried—then laughed.
4. A minstrel asked to sing about "Frodo of the Nine Fingers and the Ring of Doom."
5. Merry and Pippin
6. oliphaunts

The Steward and the King
1. She wanted to join the armies heading for Mordor.
2. by allowing him to look at/be with her: "Then, Eowyn of Rohan, I say to you that you are beautiful. In the valleys of our hills there are flowers fair and bright, and maidens fairer still; but neither flower nor lady have I seen till now in Gondor so lovely, and so sorrowful. It may be that only a few days are left ere darkness falls upon our world, and when it comes I hope to face it steadily; but it would ease my heart, if while the Sun yet shines, I could see you still."
3. Faramir milked Merry for as much information about Éowyn as he can learn.
4. Faramir and Éowyn held hands, he kissed her on her forehead and news came from a great eagle that the Dark Tower was thrown down.

Answers

5. either because it was not Aragorn who sent for her or because she didn't want to leave Faramir
6. He said, "I would," then Faramir took her in his arms and kissed her.
7. Ioreth
8. The Crown was shaped like helmets of the Guards of the Citadel. It was tall, and it had two wings shaped like a sea-bird's representing the Kings who had come across the Sea. The wings were made of pearl and silver and the Crown was set with seven diamonds around the base and a red jewel on top. Gandalf
9. The King showed mercy, and Beregond became the Captain of the Guard of Faramir, called the White Company.
10. "And he climbed to it, and saw that out of the very edge of the snow there sprang a sapling tree no more than three foot high. Already it had put forth young leaves long and shapely, dark above and silver beneath, and upon its slender crown it bore one small cluster of flowers whose white petals shone like the sunlit snow." Aragorn saw on that mount a remnant of the White Tree, whose lineage could be traced all the way back to Telperion, one of the Trees of Valinor.
11. Aragorn and Arwen were married—on Midsummer's Eve (the day between the end of June and the beginning of July).

Many Partings and *Homeward Bound*

1. She offered Frodo her place on a ship sailing to the Undying Lands and gave him "... a white gem like a star that lay upon her breast hanging upon a silver chain, and she set the chain about Frodo's neck. 'When the memory of the fear and the darkness troubles you,' she said, 'this will bring you aid.'"
2. Éomer still insisted that Galadriel was not the fairest lady that lives, but since he designated Arwen as the fairest, Gimli forgave him, because the King of Rohan had chosen the Morning while Gimli had chosen the Evening.
3. Aragorn bequeathed to Ghân-buri-Ghân and the Drûgin the Forest of Drúadan.
4. Éomer gave Gondor his sister for their prince Faramir, and Éowyn asked Aragorn to wish her joy.
5. an ancient horn that came from the hoard of Scatha the Worm
6. in a contest of words—describing the beauty of

the caves
7. at Orthanc following their visit with Treebeard
8. to send word if they heard any news of the Entwives
9. He warned them they would "find things less good in the Southfarthing."
10. the account of the crowning and marriage of Aragorn
11. Bilbo gave Frodo Sting, the mithril-coat and three books of lore; to Sam he gave a small bag of Smaug's gold; to Merry and Pippin he gave beautiful pipes made by the elves.
12. Five. Three big folk and two hobbits.
13. news that Strider was the King
14. reuniting with Bill
15. Tom Bombadil

The Scouring of the Shire

1. Bill Ferny
2. Calling the Chief Names, Wishing to Punch his Pimply Face, and Thinking the Shirriffs looked like a lot of Tom-fools
3. Lotho Sackville-Baggins
4. visit Rosie Cotton
5. Pimple (Lotho Sackville-Baggins) had the Old Mill knocked down and built an ugly red-brick mill in its place. It was full of wheels and outlandish contraptions, and polluted the stream. When Sharkey (Saruman) came to the Shire it stopped grinding corn and only poured out noise, smoke, and filth.
6. Pippin brought one hundred hobbits from Tuckborough, and they joined two hundred hobbits in Bywater. When the ruffians turned up the Bywater Road they were stopped by overturned carts. From the hedges above the men, the hobbits appeared. Merry ordered the men to lay down their weapons but the men tried to break free and fight back instead. In the end seventy ruffians were killed—with Merry killing their leader—and nineteen hobbits were killed and thirty were wounded.
7. They had cut down the Party Tree.
8. Frodo showed Saruman mercy.
9. Grima killed Lotho in his sleep. Then after Wormtongue killed Saruman, hobbit bowmen shot the former chief advisor to King Théoden of Rohan.
10. "To the dismay of those that stood by, about the body of Saruman a grey mist gathered, and rising

slowly to a great height like smoke from a fire, as a pale shrouded figure it loomed over the Hill. For a moment it wavered, looking to the West; but out of the West came a cold wind, and it bent away, and with a sigh dissolved into nothing."

Project—Restoring the Shire
In *Ents, Elves and Eriador: The Environmental Vision of J.R.R. Tolkien,* Matthew Dickerson and Jonathan Evans write:

[Wendell] Berry concludes "The Pleasure of Eating" with seven recommendations for eating responsibly. In summary, they are: (1) participate in food production to the extent you can; (2) prepare your own food; (3) know the origins of the food you buy, and buy food produced close to your home; (4) deal directly with local farmers, gardeners, or orchardists whenever possible; (5) learn as much as possible about the economy and technology of industrial food production; (6) be aware of what is involved in the best farming and gardening practices; and (7) learn as much as you can about the life histories of food species. Berry believes eating should be "an extensive pleasure." People who "know the garden in which their vegtables have grown and know the garden is healthy" will also "remember the beauty of growing plants." He continues, "Eating with the fullest pleasure—pleasure, that is, that does not depend on ignorance—is perhaps the profoundest enactment of our connection with the world. In this pleasure we experience and celebrate our dependence and our graditude, for we are living from mystery, from creatures we did not make and powers we cannot comprehend." Berry's views here echo the highest principles defining the culture of the Shire; his recommendations suggest that . . . [we]: *eat like a Hobbit,* if not in quantity, at least in quality.

The Grey Havens
1. Before removing the new mill they restored Bagshot Row, renaming it New Row.
2. Sam went all around the Shire planting saplings, and with each he put a grain of the dust in the soil at the root of each. He planted the *mallorn* seed where the Party Tree had stood.
3. Sam married Rosie Cotton.
4. *Elanor,* after the golden flower in Lothlórien
5. Gildor, Elrond and Galadriel riding with Bilbo

Baggins toward the Grey Havens.
6. Círdan the Shipwright. Círdan was a lord of the Teleri in Middle-earth, Lord of the Falas during much of the First Age, and founder of Mithlond. A *bearded* elf, Círdan was the original bearer of the Great Ring Narya, before giving it to Gandalf.
7. "I will not say: do not weep; for not all tears are an evil."

Project
1. The movie skips their negotiating with the Wild Men of Drúadan Forest for passage through their woods.
2. Faramir and Merry
3. In the book, Gandalf counsels King Elessar and shows him where to find a seedling of the White Tree.
4. In the book there is no break in the hobbit's trust, except for a brief instant in the Orc tower when Frodo demands the return of the Ring.
5. The women and children of Minas Tirith were evacuated to the countryside.
6. The Walls of Minas Tirith crumble whenever they're struck by massive rocks hurled by the Orcish army and their catapults.
7. In the book the Mouth of Sauron is allowed to live until the battle.
8. In the film, Denethor refuses to light the beacon of Minas Tirith, so Gandalf persuades Pippin to sneak past the guards and light it.
9. the Rangers of the North
10. Gollum bites the ring off Frodo's index finger (not his third finger as in the book), and Frodo charges and jumps on Gollum, causing them both to fall.
11. The Scouring of the Shire and Saruman's death there at the hands of Wormtongue.

Appendix A
1. The "mightiest in skill of word and hand" and "the greatest of the Eldar in arts and lore," Fëanor—the oldest son of Finwë, the High King of the Noldor.
2. The Ban of the Valar: the Numenoreans were forbidden to sail west out of sight of their own shore or to attempt to set foot on the Undying Lands. Sauron used the Númenor's murmuring against the Ban to fan the flames of the rebellion which brought the ruin of Tolkien's "Atlantis."

THE LORD OF THE RINGS
Answers

From Letter No. 257: "... What I might call my Atlantis-haunting. This legend or myth or dim memory of some ancient history has always troubled me. In sleep I had the dreadful dream of the ineluctable Wave, either coming out of the quiet sea, or coming in towering over the green inlands. It still occurs occasionally, though now exorcized by writing about it. It always ends by surrender, and I awake gasping out of deep water. I used to draw it or write bad poems about it. When C.S. Lewis and I tossed up, and he was to write on space-travel and I on time-travel, I began an abortive book of time-travel of which the end was to be the presence of my hero in the drowning of Atlantis. This was to be called Númenor, *the Land in the West."*

3. "Sauron lied to the King, declaring that everlasting life would be his who possessed the Undying Lands, and that the Ban was imposed only to prevent the Kings of Men from surpassing the Valar." Then when Ar-Pharazôn set foot on the shores of the Undying Lands the Valar called upon Eru and the One sank the invasion fleet and all of Númenor, separating the Undying Lands from Middle-earth.
4. Frodo was imprisoned there after visiting Tom.
5. Rivendell
6. Aragorn bound himself to his own law that no Big People were allowed to pass the borders into the Shire.
7. Elanor, the first child of Master Samwise Gamgee and his wife Rose Cotton. She was called "the Fair" for her golden hair. She became a maid of honor to Queen Evenstar in 1436. Elanor and her line after her were the keepers of the Red Book of Westmarch.
8. Tarondor, Telemnar's nephew replanted a seedling in the citadel.
9. Pelendur. Arvedui's claim was dismissed because the Council of Gondor said that the rule of Gondor belonged to the heirs of Anárion (the brother of Isildur). So they chose Eärnil as King, in spite of the Númenórean law of succession.
10. the White Tree died
11. Thorongil
12. looking into the palantír
13. Aragorn and Arwen. When Arwen returned to Rivendell in 2951 to visit her father, she met Aragorn as he walked alone one day in the woods singing.
14. She was only allowed to marry a man if he were the King of Gondor and Arnor.
15. on Cerin Amroth
16. Felaróf; Shadowfax
17. finding the Stone and building up a power of his own
18. by riding off into battle alongside King Elessar
19. the awakening/releasing of the balrog
20. Azog, the father of Bolg killed him and branded his name on the forehead of Thrór.
21. When Thorin's shield was broken he used a tree branch to defend himself.
22. Gimli; he was allowed to go with Legolas over the Sea

Appendix B
1. The Wizards of Middle-earth—a small group of immortals resembling men but possessing much greater physical and mental power, sent from the Far West to contest the power of Sauron and unite those who would resist him.
2. Círdan the Shipwright; to rekindle hearts in a world that grows chill
3. Celeborn—and even Galadriel came forth and "threw down its walls and laid bare its pits."
4. Sam became mayor, and Pippin married Diamond of Long Cleeve
5. Éomer and Éowyn
6. Pippin becomes Took and Thain
7. Sam gave Elanor the Red Book and then passed over the Sea to the Grey Havens.
8. Gondor

VOCABULARY
Book One
imbibe: To drink or absorb
provender: Dry food, such as hay, used as feed for livestock
coppice: A thicket or grove of small trees or shrubs
tussocky: A clump or tuft, as of growing grass
bollard: A thick post
hoary: Gray or white with or as if with age
barrow: A large mound of earth or stones placed over a burial site
wight: A living being; a creature
russet: yellowish brown, light brown, or reddish brown
standing stone: A prehistoric monument of a class found chiefly in the British Isles and northern France, consisting of a single tall, upright megalith.

THE LORD OF THE RINGS
Answers

damask: A rich patterned fabric of cotton, linen, silk, or wool

sallow: of a sickly, yellowish color; willow

quagmire: A difficult or precarious situation; a predicament

wraith: an apparition of a living person supposed to portend his or her death

cairn: A mound of stones set up as a memorial

Book Two

panoply: A splendid or striking array

habergeon: A short, sleeveless coat of mail

chalcedony: a milky or greyish translucent to transparent quartz

carcanet: A jeweled necklace, collar, or headband

errantry: The condition of traveling or roving about, especially in search of adventure

baldric: A belt, usually of ornamented leather, worn across the chest to support a sword or bugle

tryst: an appointment to meet at a certain time and place

sylvan: of, pertaining to, or inhabiting the woods; a mythical deity or spirit of the woods

faggot: A bundle of twigs, sticks, or branches bound together

bole: The trunk of a tree

ewer: A pitcher, especially a decorative one with a base, an oval body, and a flaring spout

hythe: A small haven

fen: Low, flat, swampy land; a bog or marsh

phial: a small bottle; vial

wold: An unforested rolling plain; a moor

eyot: small island

sloe: the small, sour, blackish fruit of the blackthorn

Book Three

escarpment: A steep slope in front of a fortification

craven: cowardly; contemptibly timid; pusillanimous

splayed: To spread out or apart, especially clumsily

dingle: A small wooded valley; a dell

eyrie: The nest of a bird, such as an eagle, built on a cliff or other high place

cleave: to split or divide by or as if by a cutting blow

sedge: any rushlike or grasslike plants growing in wet places

coomb: deep hollow or valley, especially on the flank of a hill

parapet: A low protective wall or railing along the edge of a raised structure such as a roof or balcony

flotsam: Floating refuse or debris

jetsam: Discarded cargo or equipment found washed ashore

flounder: To make clumsy attempts to move or regain one's balance; to move or act clumsily and in confusion

dotard: a person, esp. an old person, exhibiting a decline in mental faculties

remonstrance: An expression of protest, complaint, or reproof, especially a formal statement of grievances

bracken: An area overgrown with ferns and shrubs

Book Four

spate: a sudden, almost overwhelming, outpouring

bight: the middle part of a rope, as distinguished from the ends; a bend or curve in the shore of a sea or river.

pinion: a gear with a small number of teeth; wing of a bird

gangrel: a wandering beggar; vagabond; vagrant

elixir: A sweetened aromatic solution

foundered: Sunk below the surface of the water

canker: a gangrenous or ulcerous sore

gorse: Any of several spiny shrubs having fragrant yellow flowers and black pods

charnel: A repository for the bones or bodies of the dead

fey: Displaying an otherworldly, magical, or fairylike aspect or quality; Fated to die soon

doughty: Marked by stouthearted courage; brave

orb: a sphere or globe

lubber: a big, clumsy, stupid person; lout; an awkward or unskilled sailor

Book Five

oast: a kiln for drying hops

byre: a barn for cows

thain: an Anglo-Saxon term for a minor noble

wroth: angry; wrathful

pyre: a pile or heap of wood or other combustible material for burning a dead body

baluster: a railing at the side of a staircase

doggrel: Crudely or irregularly fashioned verse, often humorous (also *doggerel*)

trammel: A shackle; something that restricts activity, expression, or progress; a restraint

ghyll: a ravine

feint: a movement made in order to deceive an adversary

scree: Loose rock debris covering a slope

THE LORD OF THE RINGS
Answers

Book Six
turves: layers of matted earth formed by grass and plant roots; peat
presage: a presentiment or foreboding
puissant: powerful; mighty; potent
cudgel: A short heavy stick; a club
scouring: To remove by scrubbing
grist: action of grinding, grain to be ground
weskit: a vest or waistcoat
dawdling: to waste time; idle; trifle; loiter
shale: a sedimentary rock formed by the deposition of successive layers of clay
firth: a long, narrow indentation of the seacoast

Project—Athrabeth Finrod Ah Andreth
This story was supposed to be part of *The Silmarillion.* In that "prequel" Tolkien tells about how the universe came into existence, how Elves created jewels called the Silmarils and fought over them for generations until Melkor took them away for safekeeping, but Melkor's brother Morgoth stole the Silmarils. In the end a man named Beren steals the Silmarils from Morgoth, and when the Elves try to kill him to get them back, he gives them to his son Earendil to take across the Sea and back to Heaven.

1. both are "Children of the One"
2. the One will enter the world and heal Men and the Marring; the Incarnation
3. the Fall of Man in the Garden of Eden
4. Being greater in every way than Arda, the One would shatter Arda if He tried to enter it

Project—The Philosophy of Tolkien
1. The elves have magic that is very much like an exalted art—think of Sam's "magic rope"—they seek to harmonize with Nature/Creation whereas Sauron's magic was meant to work *against* nature—to twist it and dominate it.
2. Much of our technology tries to work against nature, as well. Any technology that seeks to thwart nature should be treated with extreme caution. It may not be bad, but might lead us to some very bad ends. Whereas technology that works in harmony with nature is a better goal.
3. Gandalf: Prophet; Frodo: Priest; Aragorn: King; all of these guys "die" and come back to life: Gandalf gains life though he "passes into shadow;" Aragorn gains new life after he passes through the Paths of the Dead; Frodo finds life after he

goes to the Cracks of Doom—all of these are metaphorical deaths that lead to life.
4. By making the setting of the story in our world, Tolkien makes us invested in the outcome. He also gives the story familiarity and lets us have a sense of how the world works; it makes us feel at home in the Shire, and makes us shudder in the alien-like Mordor.
5. By making Ents, Tolkien was able to get us to see trees (and perhaps nature) in a little different light. Ents can speak and act in ways that trees cannot, and therefore, can give us an idea of what they might be "thinking." In a less direct way, we see trees as more majestic because of the Ents in much the same way that we see horses as more impressive because of Pegasus or lions more regal because of Aslan. The fictional account of these creatures causes us to have new-found awe of the actual creature.
6. Gandalf actually tells Frodo that this is the case when he says, "A mortal, Frodo, who keeps one of the Great Rings does not die, but he does not grow or gain more life, he merely continues until every last minute is a weariness . . . He fades." We also see it in the actions of characters we know to be evil or corrupted (Gollum, Saruman, Sauron, Denethor). They all desire the Ring, whereas all virtuous characters strive to shun the temptation of the Ring. They know it is a hollow life offered by the Ring that will only end in a tormented ennui. (In the *Harry Potter* books, Lord Voldemort has this kind of immortality that Dumbledore says any human should reject in favor of death). Or, to oversimplify and generalize, our world is obsessed with the Self and anything harmful to the Self is to be shunned at all costs (hence the selfishness that plagues our society). Therefore, we naturally seek to extend our lives for as long as is conceivably possible no matter the cost (we doubt any life after death, so this would make sense). We also avoid anything that may put our lives at risk or anything that may reduce our comfort or prosperity. We look only at length of life and its comforts; rarely do we take notice of the virtue to be found in our lives. It is almost inconceivable in our time (unlike in times past) that the virtuousness of our lives is far more important than its length or material prosperity. So, like Faramir, look at what the Ring offers and reject it—even if it means our deaths, as it almost did for him.

All we have to decide
is what to do with the time
that is given to us.